Mastering LinkedIn
in
7 Days or Less

Use this book to:

✓ **Find a job**
✓ **Find clients**
✓ **Be the Recognized Expert**

. . . in record time!

Jan Wallen

ISBN: 978-0-9822969-0-5
Library of Congress Control Number: 209901761

Although Selling Your Expertise LLC has researched many sources to ensure the accuracy and completeness of the information contained in this book, Selling Your Expertise LLC cannot accept any responsibility for errors, inaccuracies, omissions, or any other inconsistency herein. Any slights against people or organizations are unintentional.

Educational and motivational materials from Selling Your Expertise LLC are available at special discounts for bulk purchases.

Companies and organizations may purchase books for premiums or resale, or may arrange a custom edition by contacting the Marketing Director at the address below. For additional information, contact:

Selling Your Expertise LLC
3042 Rt. 32
Saugerties, NY 12477
www.LinkedInWorks.com
Phone: (877) 327-5058
e-mail: info@linkedinworks.com

Creative work by Imagine That!, www.ImagineThat.com

Dedication

This book is dedicated to several of the people who have influenced my life in many ways.

To my parents: To my mother, who is always an inspiration, especially at the age of 93. You have developed and encouraged my creativity, given me an appreciation of the quality of life, and give me so much pleasure in art, drawing and watercolor. I treasure the time we spend together. To my father, who gave me a real appreciation of music, overseas travel, architecture and design. Your outlook on life and advice about how the world works was practical and right on target in the real world. I think of you both every day.

To Tom Redmond, who reminds me every now and again how sailing took me to the decision to start my business and how important that's been to me.

To Gene Smith, who makes things that are very important to me possible. To Helen Hirschfeld and Henrietta Mueller. I think of you every day.

To Gus Pedersen, with his never-ending enthusiasm, great ideas, thought-provoking questions and perspective, solid engineering with an artistic edge, and encouragement.

To Jerry and Iris Vass and Howard Camber, who introduced me to the art of *Soft Selling in a Hard World*™ many years ago. It is always with me.

To many people in my network, you've influenced me
more than you may realize.
And I thank you.

About Jan

Jan Wallen is a Business ROI Analyst, and a sales and LinkedIn expert who shows executives and business owners how to use LinkedIn to find clients and find a job … in record time. And Jan shows companies how they can save as much as 20% of the cost of sales when they use LinkedIn to find and engage their best clients. Jan is in demand for her analytical ability, vision and strategic thinking. And her hands-on, energetic and interactive style gives her clients and audiences real-time results. You want Jan on your team. Call her now to see how she can get results for you.

Jan has helped thousands of professionals find success in their business and their careers. Whether you're a CEO, executive, salesperson or entrepreneur, Jan's practical, positive approach and strategies give you all the tools, inspiration and confidence to use LinkedIn to find clients and find a job … in record time. In her LinkedIn Works! programs, Jan shows you how to use LinkedIn to do what you want to do. If you're a salesperson or business owner, you want to know how to use LinkedIn for to find clients - for prospecting and lead generation. If you're looking for a job, you want to use LinkedIn to conduct your job search. That's exactly what Jan shows you.

Jan has more than 20 years experience in sales, sales management and sales technology (CRM – Customer Relationship Management) with Fortune 500 and Big 5 firms. Her career has been working with, advising, mentoring, selling to and training C-level executives, partners, managers and business owners. She managed a national selling skills program for partners and senior consultants at PricewaterhouseCoopers, and implemented a CRM system there. She has mentored people who have left their corporate careers and started consulting businesses. Jan's business and sales experience mean that she knows how to apply proven strategies and tools like LinkedIn to impact a company's top and bottom lines. And to implement them.

The mechanics of LinkedIn are simple enough. You join, create your LinkedIn Profile, connect with people you know, and request and give Recommendations. It's the **strategies** for using LinkedIn to build your business and find a job that can be challenging. That's exactly what Jan shows you in her LinkedIn Profile Makeovers, Strategy Sessions, Webinars and hands-on seminars. Go to www.LinkedInWorks.com to choose the best way to get the results you want.

Mastering LinkedIn in 7 Days or Less – Day by Day

- Your LinkedIn Philosophy – Quality Network or Open Network?
- Your Purpose for LinkedIn
- Review this book – Plan your strategies
- Go to www.linkedin.com and join or login
- Quick Review of the Home Screen to get your bearings
- Insider Secrets
- Action Steps for Tomorrow

- Not backwards-oriented like a resume
- Search engines find you LinkedIn Profile
- Insider Secrets
- Success Stories
- Action Steps for Tomorrow

- Review your LinkedIn Profile
- Edit and Add to your Profile
- Personalize the link to your Profile
- Find people you know, look at their Profiles, get ideas
- Add to your list of people to connect with
- Insider Secrets
- Success Stories
- Action Steps for Tomorrow

Introduction and Where to Start

Hello and Welcome! You're about to learn how to use a powerful way to network online. It really works! Here are a few of the things that you can do with LinkedIn:

- Find clients, decision-makers, hiring managers
- Find your next position, a new career
- Find your next superstar employee
- Find and connect with colleagues and classmates you've lost touch with
- Find a mentor
- Find funding for your business
- Find speakers for your events and programs
- Find Guest Experts for your teleseminars
- Find people to interview for your book
- Build your brand
- Establish your status as an Expert in your field
- Recession-proof your business
- Save as much as 20% of the cost of sales
- Streamline your sales as much as 25%

. . . and many, many more.

LinkedIn is a powerful tool for business people to have in your toolbox for success, whether you're looking for a job, looking for more of your best clients or building your Expert status and brand.

I first started using LinkedIn when someone I knew invited me to be a part of their network. I looked around a bit at the LinkedIn Home page, though didn't do much with LinkedIn. Then a few months later, someone else invited me to join. I accepted. And again did nothing with LinkedIn for months. Then I read about it again and it piqued my curiosity. A few days later, a colleague who said it was one of the best tools he'd ever used gave me a brief tutorial. I was hooked! And I realized immediately how powerful LinkedIn is. My sales, marketing, networking, finding joint venture partners and clients are all much easier and more fun because of LinkedIn. And I spend less time and get better results than I did in the times before LinkedIn.

Now when I talk to people about LinkedIn, many of them started out the same way I did. They joined and didn't use it much because they didn't have time and didn't know what to do with it. So I decided to write this book. You'll find as you read this book, in my articles, eColumn, teleseminars and Webinars, when you hear me speak and talk to me, that I'm a LinkedIn Evangelist. I don't see how I ever lived without it.

Mastering LinkedIn in 7 Days or Less is not a high-tech book for high-tech people. It's the opposite. It's for busy executives and business owners who don't have a lot of time, and who want to get results *now*. I cut through all the extraneous material and tell you only what you must know to get results with LinkedIn for:

- Lead generation and prospecting
- Product and service development
- Strategic alliances, business partnerships and joint ventures and consulting opportunities
- Preparation for sales calls and visits – never cold call again
- Helping people in your network find jobs and clients
- Building your brand, and
- Establishing your status as an Expert

Here you have day-by-day steps that take only 15-20 minutes. You *can* be successful with LinkedIn in only 15-20 minutes a day. You may spend more at times when you're looking for a job or stepping up your sales and marketing efforts. At other times, 15-20 minutes regularly and consistently gets results.

Two chapters in this book allow for more than 15-20 minutes to get started. Thinking about how you want to use LinkedIn and approach your online networking, and creating your LinkedIn Profile take a little longer. If you don't have time to spend 20-30 minutes doing those completely now, that's OK. Get started, and go back to it at a later time.

Pick your Track

This book shows you how to get results and ROI with LinkedIn, whether you're a new member or more experienced. To get the most from the book, pick a track from the ones here, and follow it.

I'm New to LinkedIn, and Want to Start Using It More – Choose this one if you've joined and haven't done much with LinkedIn since you joined, or if you use other social networking sites and aren't sure what LinkedIn can do for you

- Start with the FAQs in Appendix A: Articles
- Take time with the *Night Before . . .* chapter, and write down notes and your answers
- Go through the book day by day, following the steps each day
- Do the Action Steps for Tomorrow each day with your real-life examples
- Start using it almost every day for a few minutes with your real-life searches and connections
- I'm looking for people to interview for my next books about the best ways to get started with LinkedIn, success stories and new ways people are using LinkedIn. Send an e-mail to me at: info@linkedinworks.com and put "New" in the Subject line.

I'm Already Using LinkedIn, and Want to use it More Effectively – Choose this one if you've started using LinkedIn and like it, though you don't see a lot of success yet, or don't feel comfortable and confident about using it

- Glance at the FAQs in Appendix A: Articles
- Scan the *Night Before . . .* chapter, and write down notes and your answers
- Scan the Days chapters to see if you've done these steps when you use LinkedIn, are comfortable doing them, and are doing them pretty quickly now
- Find something you're not doing as quickly or thoroughly as you'd like, and start with that chapter.
- Take time reading the Articles, especially *10 Ways You Never Thought of Using LinkedIn*. Find ways to do these for your own goals.
- I'm looking for people to interview for my next books about the best ways to get started with LinkedIn, success stories and new ways

people are using LinkedIn. Send an e-mail to me at:
info@linkedinworks.com and put "Effective" in the Subject line.

I'm a LinkedIn Expert, and Always Want to Know More – Choose this
one if you're already using LinkedIn a lot, have success stories and advice for
people who aren't using it a lot. And you're always looking for new things to
do with LinkedIn.

- Glance at the FAQs in Appendix A: Articles, scan the *Night Before . . .*
  chapter, and write down notes and your answers. Scan the Days
  chapters to see if you've done these steps as you've used LinkedIn, are
  comfortable doing them, and are doing them quickly as you use
  LinkedIn. Start with a chapter if you see something that's new.
- Read the Articles, especially *10 Ways You Never Thought of Using
  LinkedIn!* Find ways to do these for your own goals.
- I'm looking for people to interview for my next books about the best
  ways to get started with LinkedIn, success stories and new ways
  people are using LinkedIn. Send an e-mail to me at:
  info@linkedinworks.com and put "Expert" in the Subject line.

Mastering LinkedIn in 7 Days or Less will get you started making LinkedIn
work for you without spending a lot of time doing it. You can do the
activities listed in this plan in about 15-20 minutes a day. Part of the key to
making LinkedIn work is to use it almost every day, even for a few minutes.
You don't have to set aside blocks of time to learn it or to make it work for
you. In fact, if you're already committed to networking, this tool makes is
even easier to do what you're already doing.

You have Action Steps each day for ways to network, so you really connect
and network rather simply collecting LinkedIn Profiles like a stack of business
cards from a networking meeting.

To make the most of LinkedIn, make it a habit to go to LinkedIn every day or
every other day, especially when you first start using it. When you're learning
something new, it takes longer the first few times you do it. So when you go
to LinkedIn every day, you'll learn and remember faster.

Start a folder called "LinkedIn". Put your notes, articles you come across, and
lists of people you want to connect with in one place. Keep it handy.

I decided to write this book because many times when I've discovered a new technology or tool to use, so many of the books are excruciatingly long and technical, and try to give you a quick helicopter tour that doesn't show you how to apply the tool to your own situation and goals. I'm busy. I'm action- and results-oriented, and don't have a lot of time to learn new tools. **I want to learn what will help me and I want results *now*!** That is, I want to know the essence of the tool, what it can do for me, and the basics so I'm up and running as soon as possible.

My philosophy has always been, "You don't have to know how the engine works to drive a car" and "Why wait? -- Get results today." It's the same whether it's with technology tools or driving a car. I want to drive the car, not know everything that goes on under the hood. That's why I wrote this book.

You'll be using LinkedIn for yourself by the time you finish this book, even if you haven't joined yet. If you want to be more confident and want to ask me questions, join one of my teleseminars or live LinkedIn events. Schedule a LinkedIn Strategy Session with me if you want to accomplish something with LinkedIn and aren't quite sure how to approach it. Or sign up for a LinkedIn Profile Makeover, ongoing coaching or the monthly Quick-Start Coaching. Simply click on the link below or type it into your browser to find out more and sign up: www.linkedinworks.com/store.htm

To be successful in networking and with LinkedIn, it takes practice and a commitment to using it consistently. It doesn't take a lot of time. You can be successful in networking with LinkedIn if you spend 15-20 minutes a day consistently.

My clients have frequently asked me how I started using LinkedIn and how I became a LinkedIn Evangelist.

My own personal and professional situation points up the value of LinkedIn in a way that I might not have noticed if I lived in a different location and situation. My career was in sales, sales management and sales technology (CRM – Customer Relationship Management) with Fortune 500 and Big 5 firms -- working with, selling to and training C-level executives, partners, senior consultants, managers and staff. I managed a national selling skills program for partners and senior consultants at PricewaterhouseCoopers, and implemented a CRM (Customer Relationship Management) system there. I was a top producer in sales in Chicago and New York selling an accurate database of executives that companies used for their marketing. I lived overseas in Germany, London (UK), Okinawa (Japan) and Rotterdam (The Netherlands), and traveled to all the surrounding countries.

Now I live in the beautiful Hudson Valley, a rural area north of New York (city). I'm now in a very small community, so a lot of my connections with my clients and my network are via the telephone and Internet. That's where LinkedIn comes in and is so valuable. LinkedIn is the premier online network for business people. Where I live now there aren't many corporate or business people to meet with, and there are great distances between companies and networking meetings. My Networking Principle #3 below (*Go where the fish are*) outlines a critical reason why I'm such a LinkedIn Evangelist.

So I'm networking with LinkedIn, and connecting with people, reaching goals, finding clients and joint venture partners and alliances, and helping people in my network find jobs. The people in my network are all a part of my Success Team. In a word, LinkedIn is the lifeline for my business.

Everywhere we are we have real-life social networks, business networks and career networks. They may be networks that other people have created, or that exist as a part of institutions and customs in the area. Or you can develop your own network. For example, social networks include book clubs, church groups, social clubs, hiking clubs, cultural and recreation groups. You meet people with common interests, and socialize, contribute and learn from each other. Business and career groups are more focused on doing business and career activities.

Now we also have online social, business and career networks. Online social networks include: Facebook, MySpace, YouTube, Twitter, and many more. LinkedIn is the premier online network for business. These networks are not only popular. Many companies are hiring people to track social networking, and expecting their employees to be adept at using these social networking sites, especially if your job requires outreach. If your job requires outreach, you're expected to use LinkedIn and social networking.

I invite you to tell me what I can do to help you and to advance your networking. Send an e-mail to me at: info@linkedinworks.com and put Let's Network in the Subject line. I welcome your ideas, connections and advice, and welcome your calls and connections on LinkedIn. Send an e-mail to me at: info@linkedinworks.com and put My Ideas in the Subject line.

It's no wonder that LinkedIn Works!

The Night Before Day 1
20-30 minutes

The Night Before Day 1 – Preparation – 20-30 minutes

Starting with these steps will give you a Quick Start with LinkedIn and the activities you'll do tomorrow and every day this week. And it will mean that you spend less time on a day-to-day basis using LinkedIn because you'll set up your Profile so it's designed to achieve the results you want and serve your purpose for being on LinkedIn.

A project management Rule of Thumb is, "10 minutes of pre-planning saves 10 hours of time and hassle later on". It's the same with LinkedIn. Take a few minutes now to read this chapter and answer the questions. Jot notes down. They're you're initial ideas, and will likely change by the time you reach the end of the book and are using LinkedIn.

Step 1 – Your LinkedIn Purpose: What do You Want LinkedIn to Do for You?

1. **Start a folder or hanging folder called "LinkedIn".** Put it in a place where it's always at your fingertips.

2. **Have your resume handy.** Review it, and be sure it's up-to-date and written in a results-oriented way. If you're conducting a job search, be sure it shows what you're looking for in your next position, and how your company (or department) was different after you worked there. If you're looking for clients, describe your services and show the benefits for your clients. You can do this in a story format where you paint a picture in the mind of the reader that shows the situation when a client called you in, how you approached the challenges, and how it was different after your client worked with you. Update it with your current position and work. You'll use this as the basis for your LinkedIn Profile. Your Profile is the key to being found on LinkedIn. You can't do anything in LinkedIn until you have your Profile up. You'll create your Profile tomorrow.

3. **Read the article *10.5 Ways to Optimize your LinkedIn Profile* in** Appendix A of this book. Look at your resume and make notes about things in your resume to expand on for your LinkedIn Profile.

4. **Make notes about what you want to get from using LinkedIn.** What are your goals? Are you looking for a new position? New clients? Do you want to establish your status as an Expert? Or build your company brand? Find your next superstar employee? LinkedIn does all of these. Be clear on what you want to do with LinkedIn. Write your notes here:

5. **Write down the area(s) you want to be known as the Expert in.** Write your strengths and areas of expertise. As you use LinkedIn more and more, devote time often to asking and especially answering questions in the Answers section of LinkedIn. This gives you visibility and the opportunity to build Expert status in your field. Write what you want to be known as the Expert in here.

6. **Reviewing your business plan or company vision** may be helpful in clarifying your goals and what you want LinkedIn to do for you. The Big Picture Worksheet is outlined below. It's something I use with my clients to clarify their goals and thinking during the year. It's brief, and gives you a snapshot of your current situation and goals.

Think about both your personal and professional goals and how you want LinkedIn to help you achieve them. You can also get a copy of the Big Picture Worksheet by simply clicking on the link below or typing it into your browser:
www.linkedinworks.com/resources/bigpicture.pdf

Take a few minutes now to write your vision of your Ideal business, career and life outside work.

The Helicopter Big Picture View of Your Business and Your Life

Step back from "real life" with all its details for a few minutes, and imagine that you're in a helicopter 50,000' above your business and your life. What do you see?

1. **Your current work situation** – Describe your career and work or business. Include your colleagues, boss, work environment, responsibilities, pressures, and the potential for promotion and salary increases. If you have a business, describe your clients, revenue, income <u>vs</u>. expenses, goals, how it's grown over the last 1-2 years, changes you'd make, things you've learned. Also think about how you want your Ideal business and life to be in 1-3 years.

2. **Your current life** – Describe your time, priorities, values, accomplishments, changes you'd make and things you've learned. What do you want it to be like in 1-3 years?

3. **Your future career or business** – Describe how you see your career or business 3 years from now. 1 year from now? 6 months? Who do you work with? What position do you hold? Who are your

colleagues outside work? Who are your clients? Where do you work?

4. **Consider the following before you create your LinkedIn Profile.** Remember, the most efficient and effective way to get started on LinkedIn is to think things through first. That way, you'll get the results you want. Jot your notes here:

- Your **Current Purpose** and what you want to accomplish with LinkedIn

- Make your Profile **results-oriented** (like a resume). What results do you want people to see?

- Make your Profile **focused on the present** and what you want to accomplish – a big mistake people make is to be backwards-focused, and emphasize their past accomplishments

- Think about **who will see your Profile**. What will they be looking for? Be sure they can find you.

- When Your Profile is completed, **LinkedIn and other search engines find your Profile based on keywords**. Think of the **keywords** that are appropriate to your situation, purpose and goals. Make a list of key words and keep the list handy so you can add more as your situation and purpose change.

  There are keyword tools to help you with keywords. Go to Google and search for "keyword tool" and you'll get a list of them. The one I use is **Google AdWords Keyword Tool.** https://adwords.google.com/select/KeywordToolExternal

To learn more about these tools and how to use them, send an e-mail to me at: info@linkedinworks.com and put Keywords in the Subject line.

Write the keywords you'll use here:

In LinkedIn you can **build your status as an Expert.** What areas do you want to be known for? In your industry? A specific Niche? Results you get? What are they? Write them here:

- **What is your networking strategy and commitment?** You can get results with LinkedIn in consistently using it for 15-20 minutes/day. You'll most likely spend more time if you're looking for a new position or in a similar situation. How much time will you spend each week?

Step 2 – What's Your Networking Philosophy?

1. **Decide what your philosophy about LinkedIn connections will be**. There are several approaches. One is the Quality Network approach where you build a network of quality connections where you know everyone you connect with. You invite people you know to be a part of your network, and you don't accept invitations from people you don't know. Another approach is the Quantity approach where you connect with as many people as possible, whether you know them or not. This approach is called Open Networking. If this is your approach, you are called a LinkedIn Open Networker (LION). When you see LION on their Profiles, that's what it means. There is no one

right way. The best approach for you is the one that fits your philosophy and goals.

2. **Join LinkedIn** if you haven't already joined. It's free to join. Go to www.linkedin.com and join. You can also upgrade your account for additional services, though I highly recommend starting with the basic program first. You can upgrade when you'll actually use the additional features. More about that later. For now, join with the free membership.

3. *IMPORTANT: If you don't have your LinkedIn Profile up yet, you won't see some of the features in this Orientation section, so start your Profile with your name and current work.*

   Fill in your contact information, name, geographic area and your current position. Don't take a lot of time doing this now; we'll create your Profile tomorrow, and I'll give you lots of tips.

4. **Read the LinkedIn Terms of Service** (As of this writing, this is available on the LinkedIn Web site: www.LinkedIn.com. Abide by them as you network with LinkedIn. Your account can be terminated and you may not be able to sign up again if you don't abide by the Terms of Service.

Step 3 – Orientation: Join and Decide who to Connect With

1. **Start a list of people you want to connect with.** Keep adding names to your list every day or so. Put your list where you can easily add names and refer to your list when you're on LinkedIn and can invite them to connect.

2. **Explore and find people you know who are LinkedIn members.** Go to "People" at the top left of the LinkedIn Home page. Type in the first and last names of people you know who might be LinkedIn members. When you find them, notice their Profiles. You'll be creating your Profile tomorrow. Get an idea of what Profiles are like and ideas for creating yours. Think of your purpose, and then find people you know and look at their Profiles. Click on **People** at the top left of the screen, and type in their first and last names to search.

Step 4 – Orientation: Your LinkedIn Home Page

Go to www.linkedin.com and login. You'll go to your Home Page when you sign in. Look at your Home page as you go through this section of the book. If you don't have your LinkedIn Profile up yet, you won't see some of these features. Start your Profile with your name, geographic area, industry and current position.

NOTE: Your screen may look somewhat different from my screen, which is shown in the following pages. You'll see the basic sections described here.

Home Page

Here's what my Home Page looks like when the book was published. It may not be exactly like what you see, and LinkedIn may have changed the page after the book was published. If this is not what you see on your LinkedIn Home Page (that is, when you first sign on to LinkedIn in the morning), send an e-mail to me at info@linkedinworks.com with Home Page in the Subject line. Tell me how yours is different. We'll make the changes in the next version of this book.

Top Area – for Searches

Look at the white bar -- the top inch across the screen from left to right. This area appears all the time – no matter what you're doing in LinkedIn. You can always start new searches from here, and at the very top, you can find Help, see and change your Account and Settings, and Logout. Starting at the left side, you'll see:

People – Searches for people start here. For example, look for people you know so you can invite them to connect and be a part of your LinkedIn network. Look for people you don't know yet who may be clients, joint venture partners, strategic alliances, mentors, or who can introduce you to people you want to know.

Jobs – Job searches start here. You'll also find Tips for Finding Jobs with LinkedIn. You can search by Keywords, Country and Postal Code, and do an Advanced Job Search. If you're an employer looking for your next superstar employee, you can post your job from here.

Answers – You can ask and answer questions here. Come here and ask and answer questions frequently when you're building your brand and establishing your status as an Expert.

Companies – Company searches start here. For example, you can search by Industry, Country and Postal Code (and even look up the Zip code if you don't know it – LinkedIn makes it so easy!). The information you find in Company searches is comprehensive, including a description, size, headquarters area, number of employees, divisions, career paths for employees there, which employees there are most connected to others in LinkedIn, employees who are on LinkedIn, new hires, recent promotions and popular profiles. And you can see the icons that show if people at that company are 1st level connections , 2nd or 3rd level connections.

1st **level** connections are when you know someone at that company.

2nd **level** connections are when your connections know someone at that company

3rd **level** connections are when the connections of your connections know someone at that company

Service Providers – You'll see this at the far right of the screen after you click on Companies. You can look for service providers who have been recommended by people who have used their services. You can also recommend service providers you've worked with, and these recommendations are welcomed. Service Providers are companies that other LinkedIn members have recommended.

Left Columns – Your Home Base

Look at the left column going down the screen from top to bottom. This area appears all the time – no matter what you're doing in LinkedIn. You can always go back Home from here. From the top, you can go to:

- LinkedIn Groups
- Your Profile
- Contacts
- Your Inbox and
- Applications. Applications are third-party applications that work with LinkedIn and that enable you to enrich your Profile, share and collaborate with your network, and get insights that help you be more effective. They're added to your homepage and Profile so you can control who has access to what information. For example, as I'm writing this, these are some of the applications: Huddle Workspaces, Google Presentation, Company Buzz, Box.net Files, SlideShare Presentations, Blog Link, My Travel and WordPress. LinkedIn is always improving and enhancing its services, so this list is likely to become out of date, and not be the same as what you see now on your screen. You can always see the current applications on your Home page.

Below this "Home" box, you'll see a box where you can see your photo and the professional headline from your LinkedIn Profile. Scroll down to see **how many connections** you have, how many new connections have been added to your network. You can also let your network know what you're working on. Simply click on the words "What Are Your Working On?" at the bottom of this section, and type in a few words, then click Save. To choose who sees this, click on the tiny [Edit] at the right. It can be visible to only your Network, or to Everyone.

Center of the Screen – Your Inbox and Building your Network

If you looked at any of the features above, go back to "Home" now – Click on *Home* in the top left are of your screen, near the top.

LinkedIn gives you several ways to check your Inbox easily, and **build your network** here. For example, you can check your Inbox and take the appropriate actions (read messages, archive messages, or take action on messages).

Your **Inbox** shows messages waiting for you. Some may be pending action, some may be ready to archive, and some may be unread. Check your Inbox regularly and take the appropriate action.

Network Updates

Network Updates is a very interesting section to review. And it's a way to make LinkedIn, which is so huge, more manageable. I highly recommend reviewing it daily because it keeps you up-to-date with what's happening in your network and the people that others in your network are connected to. You'll see who in your network is connected with others. These may also be good connections for you, so you may want to be in touch and start to build a relationship. Check them out – it may mean your next job, new clients, a mentor, or simply a good connection for the future. And *pick up the phone* if it makes sense. People seldom so that, and the person on the other end usually loves to connect with a phone call.

You'll see network connections from **Today**, **Yesterday**, **Groups** you belong to, other Groups, and who **Just Joined LinkedIn** from companies you work for or worked for, and classmates from schools you attended. You can click on the company or school name and see who's just joined. If you know them, invite them to be a part of your network. If you don't know them, check them out and invite them if they are a good fit for your network.

Here's one of my **Insider Secrets** about these Network Updates: Scan them every day, and see who's connected to whom. The way I look at it, LinkedIn is bringing a list of connections right to you. You don't even have to make the effort to do a search. While every connection you see here may not be a good one for you, chances are that someone you know will connect with another like-minded person. You'll find a new connection that you'd never have found in a search. And you can start your networking relationship by saying that you, too, are connected with the person you both know. It's a good ice breaker.

Right Side of the Screen – Items of Interest

This is one of the most interesting areas of LinkedIn. You'll see different things here at different times when you login.

These Modules can be changed, edited or deleted so you see exactly what you want to see here. For information on how to change these modules, check out LinkedIn Help.

People You May Know

At the top right, you'll see "People You May Know". LinkedIn searches the Profiles and shows you people you may know from companies, school or geographic areas. You see their name and company, and can click on their name to see their LinkedIn Profile.

Interesting people always pop up here – including myself! Here's an **Insider Secret**: If you see someone here that you want to connect with, either connect right away, or write down the person's name. You may not see it again for a while.

Check out the "People you May Know" area every day. Add people to your network if you know them, and look at the Profiles of people you don't know. See if they fit your purpose for being in LinkedIn, will be a good addition to your network (and you a good addition to theirs), and you can both help each other by networking. Invite the ones that fit to be a part of your network. You can do that right from here.

If you do invite someone from here, you can continue to find more people you know and invite them without going back to the Home page or doing a People search.

Tip: Your Home Page is always a good place to start or go back to, if you lose track of where you are, or don't find what you're looking for.

Featured Applications in LinkedIn

Applications make it possible for you to collaborate on projects, get key insights, and present your work to the LinkedIn network (the world's largest professional network). One is featured each day. You can customize these applications.

Who's Viewed my Profile

This shows you how many people have viewed your Profile, and how often you've appeared in search results. If you're not appearing a great deal, you may want to fine-tune your Profile. For example, add or change keywords, and describe your responsibilities in more detail. Remember that people are searching for people who meet their criteria.

Reading List by Amazon

Here you can **create a reading list** for yourself, share what you're reading with your network, look at other peoples' lists, and see who's looking at your list.

- **Network Updates** – see what people in you network are reading

- **Industry Updates** – see what people in your industry are reading

- **All Updates** –

Events

You see a list of events of interest here. You can:

- list an event
- tell people that you're attending, presenting or exhibiting at an event
- notify your network about an event
- promote the event –
- display attendance at events, and much more

Answers

This area shows you a few of the questions that have been asked in a category. When you click on one of the questions, you go to that question. You can see any answers that are there, and you can answer it or suggest an Expert. You can also go to the Profile of the person who's asked the question or answered the question.

LinkedIn shows you a few questions related to your industry. To see more questions in that category, click on **See more. . .** If you want to browse questions and answers in all categories, look for "Browse all" when you scroll down below the Answers.

Jobs

LinkedIn shows you a few jobs available that are related to your industry. To see more jobs in this category, click on. **See more . . .** You'll see a complete description of the job, skills required, who posted it, and you can apply for it right there. At the bottom, you can also see related jobs.

Insider Secrets:

1. Check out the "**People you May Know**" area every day. Add people to your network if you know them, and look at the Profiles of people you don't know. See if they fit your purpose for being in LinkedIn, will be a good addition to your network (and you a good addition to

theirs), and you can both help each other by networking. Invite the ones that fit to be a part of your network. You can do that right from here.

2. Scroll down on the Home page and **check your Inbox for action items,** and take the appropriate action. This gives you reminders that you may have forgotten about.

3. Take time to think about how you want to use LinkedIn, and your situation and goals. A principle of project management says, "10 minutes of planning ahead of time saves 10 hours of work."

4. LinkedIn will make your work, your sales, getting a new position and branding easier. You may be busy and think you don't have time for anything new. Success and results come when you spend as little as 15-20 minutes/day. Think of it as a productivity tool rather than "one more thing to do".

5. If you've already joined LinkedIn and haven't used it a great deal, **do not** create another account now. It's easy to sign up more than once, especially with a different e-mail address. Then some of your connections are on one account and some are on the other one. If you signed up with an e-mail address that you no longer use, you can add a new e-mail address to your account. Go to *Account & Settings* (very top right side of the screen), then *Personal Information* to add an e-mail address. Keep the old e-mail address to be sure that people can contact you.

Action Steps for Tomorrow:

1. **Scan the rest of this book** to get an overview of what's coming, so you know what to think about before you log on tomorrow. As with many things in life, if you plant the seeds the night before, the answers often come to you by morning.

2. **Read *10.5 Ways to Optimize your LinkedIn Profile*** in Appendix A, and jot notes down about points to include in your Profile when you create it tomorrow. Keep the article and your notes handy.

3. **Review your notes for what you want LinkedIn to do for you.** You may have new ideas now that you've explored the LinkedIn Home page and have an idea about a how it works. Tomorrow you'll create your Profile so that it fits your purpose and goals.

Day 1 – Create your LinkedIn Profile

30-40 minutes

DAY 1 – Create your LinkedIn Profile – 30-40 minutes

More time is devoted today to creating your Profile than the other days because your LinkedIn Profile is the cornerstone of your presence on LinkedIn. You can't do anything until you have your Profile up. It's the key to finding people and being found on LinkedIn. Your Profile is more than a resume.

In fact, **one of the biggest mistakes** many people make is simply uploading their resume to LinkedIn. Resumes are backwards oriented. They show what you've done and accomplished in the past, and how you got to where you are now. Your LinkedIn Profile is much more. It also shows **what you're doing now**, **what you want to do in the future**, your interests and who you are as a person.

Take time and thought with your Profile. It's your presence and it's a sales and marketing piece in addition to your Web site.

People are more likely to connect and network with you when they know something about who you are and what you're interested in, they can see your photo so you're more real to them, see if you're like other people they know, and get a sense of whether they'll know, like and trust you. **People do business with people they know, like and trust**, so be sure your Profile shows things that give you credibility and that you're accessible.

Remember that this is a snapshot of who you are, and people are going to get a first impression of you by reading your Profile. You don't have a second chance to make a first impression. Make it a good one.

When your Profile is completed, LinkedIn and other search engines find your Profile based on keywords. Think of the keywords that are appropriate to your situation, purpose and goals. Make a list of keywords and keep the list handy so you can add more as your situation and purpose change.

You'll start creating your Profile today, and add more to it tomorrow and most likely the next day, too. The LinkedIn Profile process is a dynamic one, and you'll change the information there periodically to reflect your current situation and goals.

In your Profile, you'll include information on:
- Your current position and past positions
- Your education
- Your Profile summary and photo
- Your Specialties
- Your Connections
- What you're looking for on LinkedIn (for example, consulting offers, new ventures, job inquiries, expertise requests, business deals, reference requests
- Recommendations that people write for you
- Additional information including your interests, Web sites, blogs, RSS feeds and other online resources you want people to see; Groups and Associations, and Honors and Awards
- Contact Settings (how you want people to contact)
- And there's a link for your Public Profile. That is, the link you can use to send people to your LinkedIn Profile.

Be sure to write your Profile to fit your current purpose and what you want to accomplish by using LinkedIn. And tell a story in the Summary section about your company and yourself, and show what you do for your clients. Weave keywords into your story. Don't put them as bullet points or a list. For example,

- If you're **looking for a job**, be sure your Profile is complete and shows the results you've achieved in your current and past positions. Make it results-oriented, like your resume. Also be sure that your Profile shows what you're doing now and what you want to do in the future. And be sure that your settings for your Public Profile allow everyone see your entire Profile. You can check this in Accounts & Settings on your LinkedIn Home page). You can change your settings later on if you want to, after you've landed that new position.

- If you're **building your business**, be sure the information in your Profile accurately describes your expertise, products and services in a compelling and results-oriented way.

- If you want to **build your personal or professional brand** as well as your visibility and credibility, be sure you answer questions in LinkedIn Answers. Be sure the ones you ask and answer show your areas of expertise.

Step 1 – Create your Profile: Enter Information

Login to LinkedIn and start at the LinkedIn Home page.

1. **If you haven't joined LinkedIn yet, go to <u>www.LinkedIn.com</u> and join.** It's free to sign up. If you've joined, sign in.

2. **Review your list of what you want LinkedIn to do for you** (from yesterday). What's your purpose for networking on LinkedIn? What's your philosophy of networking – A Quality Network or Open Network?

7. **Read the article *10.5 Ways to Optimize your LinkedIn Profile* in** Appendix A. Look at your resume and make notes about things in your resume to expand on for your LinkedIn Profile.

3. Click on ***Profile*** (top left of the Home screen) and then ***Edit Profile***. You may have already started your Profile. So today you'll add more to it.

4. **Start entering information** in each section of your Profile, starting with your current position. Be concise and clear. You can put more than one Title in the Title box and other sections, though there is a limitation on the number of characters you can use.

   It's easy to copy and paste information from your resume into the Description box. Remember that people are going to use what they read here to decide whether to contact you, invite you to connect, consider you for a job opportunity, or to do business with you. Make it compelling and personable so they'll want to contact you.

   Be sure to upload a photo. When people see a Profile without a photo, they skip right over it and go on to a Profile where they can "see" the person. This is very important.

5. **Save or Update** each section periodically. I recommend adding the information in all of the sections before you go back and edit or change what's there. Tomorrow you can make revisions, and it can be easier to see what you want when it's all there, rather than adding a line or two then editing it. This is a dynamic process, and you'll continue to revise your Profile periodically.

6. **Be sure you've saved your Profile.** Click on the Update box when you've made changes to your Profile.

Step 2 – Review your Profile

1. **Look at your Profile as people will see it on LinkedIn.** Note any changes or revisions you want to make. Make them now if you have time, or wait until tomorrow.

2. **Print out your Profile to review tomorrow.** You can do this by printing the Web page, or copying it into a Word document.

3. **Ask yourself: "If I see this Profile, will it catch my attention?** Will I want to connect with this person? Or hire them? Or do business with them?" If not, how can I make the Profile more compelling? Make notes for tomorrow.

4. **Does the information in your Profile help achieve your purpose for LinkedIn?** Will the best people contact you? Make notes for tomorrow.

Step 3 – Look at Other Peoples' Profiles

Login to LinkedIn and start at the LinkedIn Home page.

1. **Search for people you know.** For example, find colleagues from a company you work for or used to work for, and take a look at several Profiles to see what they look like. Go to "People" at the top left of the screen, and type in a name for a basic search. You'll see fields to fill in for your searches. Fill them in and you'll see a list of Profiles that match your search criteria.

2. **Look at their Profiles to see how they created theirs**, and note ways that you want to add to or change yours.

3. **Especially look at:**
   o Recommendations
   o Descriptions of current and past employment
   o Summaries

Insider Secrets:

1. **Your Profile is a sales and marketing piece** for you, whether you're representing yourself or your business. It's like your own personal Web site, too. When your Profile is completed, LinkedIn and other search engines find your Profile based on keywords. Think of the keywords that are appropriate to your situation, purpose and goals. Make a list of keywords and keep the list handy so you can add more as your situation and purpose change.

2. **There are keyword tools you can use to help you find good keywords for you.** The one I use is the Google AdWords Keyword Tool -- https://adwords.google.com/select/KeywordToolExternal.

   You can also go to Google and search for "**keyword tool**" to find several tools.

3. **People buy from and do business with people they know, like and trust.** Write your LinkedIn Profile so that it gives you **credibility** and **visibility**, and people can see that you're **accessible** and a **good addition** to their network.

4. **Network** in a way that builds a relationship and builds trust with people. Be friendly and accessible. Do what you say you'll do. Keep in touch regularly and consistently.

5. If you're not sure that your LinkedIn Profile is as effective or compelling as it could be, my **LinkedIn Profile Critique and Makeover** is perfect for you. We focus completely on your LinkedIn Profile and how to make it fit your goals. You'll receive specific recommendations and strategies, and we can even rewrite it for you. **Sign up at www.LinkedInWorks.com**

Success Story:

Guy Kawasaki, who has used LinkedIn for a long time, and has written about LinkedIn, decided to have a LinkedIn Profile Extreme Makeover, and tells about it here: http://blog.guykawasaki.com/2007/01/linkedin_profil.html

Action Steps for tomorrow:

1. **Make a list of 5-10 People to search for. Be sure to include job titles, industries, and geographic areas. You'll do searches that fit with your own goals.**

    - _____

    - _____

    - _____

    - _____

    - _____

    - _____

    - _____

    - _____

    - _____

    - _____

2. **Make a list of 5-10 Companies to search for. Be sure to include
    industries and geographic areas. You'll do searches that fit with
    your own goals.**

- _____

- _____

- _____

- _____

- _____

- _____

- _____

- _____

- _____

- _____

Day 2 – Searches

15-20 minutes

DAY 2 – Searches – 15-20 minutes

LinkedIn makes it very easy to do simple searches to find people, jobs, answers to questions you and others have asked, and companies.

With LinkedIn, you can do simple searches to find people you know who are already on LinkedIn. Or complex, advanced searches for your best clients and decision-makers who have specific titles or are in specific industries and geographic areas. And many combinations of these.

The basic searches are self-explanatory. To find people you know who are on LinkedIn, click on the word "People" at the top left of the Home screen. To search for jobs, click on "Jobs", and the same for Answers and Companies.

For the Advanced searches, LinkedIn guides you and gives you menus to choose from. Make your selections from the appropriate boxes to find the people you're looking for, either people you know who are already on LinkedIn, or people you want to connect with.

Here's an example of how you can make LinkedIn searches work for you:

Let's say you're a business owner and your company provides sales and customer service training for Information Technology (IT) consulting firms. You're located in the northeast, and are expanding your company across the U.S., starting in Chicago. You're looking for prospective clients and your decision-makers in IT consulting companies in the Chicago area.

1. Start with a **Company** search.
2. Search by **Industry**. Start typing in "information technology" and a list comes up. Choose "Information Technology and Services".
3. Fill in the **Zip Code** for the Chicago area. For example, 60601. You can even look up the Zip Code right there (see the tiny word "Lookup" below the Zip Code box. LinkedIn does amazing things!
4. Your list of companies in the IT and Services industry comes up, showing their location and number of employees.
5. Choose one and click on the Company name. You'll see the details, including employees, new hires, recent promotions and changes, and popular profiles. Several of your decision-makers are likely to be here.

6. Click on their names and you'll see their profile with their background. You determine if they're the right person for you to contact and if they are a good prospective client for you.

Result: You save a tremendous amount of time finding the right person to contact PLUS the cost of having someone in your organization research companies on a mailing list to update the list and find the current person to contact. And because you know their background once you look at their LinkedIn Profile, you know exactly how to connect with them. They may have worked with a colleague of yours, or gone to the same school you did, or you may know someone who's written a Recommendation for them. You know how to break the ice and start a conversation and a relationship.

IMPORTANT for today:

For your 15-20 minutes today, **pick the *one*** of the following searches that's most appropriate for your goals, and do that one for your 20-30 minutes today. For example, if you're looking for people to connect with on LinkedIn, choose the People search. If you're looking for a job, choose the Job search. If you're a salesperson, you may want to start with the Company search. The Answers area of LinkedIn is a good way to establish yourself as an Expert in your area of expertise and build your brand. I recommend that you start with one of the other searches for the purpose of this book and for getting the results you want with LinkedIn in 7 days or less, and explore the Answers section later on.

Another time, come back and do the other searches, so that you get the full benefit from using LinkedIn to find exactly what you're looking for.

Step 1 – Searches -- 20-30 minutes

Pick *one* of these for today – Search for People, Jobs *or* Companies

Searches start at the top of your LinkedIn screen. You'll see the Search words People, Jobs, Answers and Companies at the very top left of your screen, next to the LinkedIn logo from anywhere you are in LinkedIn. You'll also see the search box at the top right of your screen from anywhere in LinkedIn.

Notice the small arrows next to People, Jobs, Answers and Companies at the very top left. Click the small arrow next to each word, and you'll see a menu of the types of searches you can do. This is a shortcut that LinkedIn has given us. For example, if you know you want to search for Companies, click on the small arrow, and then slide your mouse down and click on **Companies**. If you're looking for a Service Provider, slide your mouse down and click on **Service Providers**.

If you know you want to Ask a question, click the small arrow, and then slide your mouse down and click on **Ask a Question**. You go right to that section.

Search for People

Login to LinkedIn and start at the LinkedIn Home page. Refer to the screen shot for People searches later in this chapter.

1. **Search for People** you know who are already LinkedIn members. Start a list of the people you want to connect with. Click on **People** at the very left top of the LinkedIn Home page (or in the box near the top to the right of your screen next to the blue button that says "Search".) You'll see the Advanced Search boxes to fill in. In the two yellow boxes on the right of the screen, type in the first and last names of the person you want to find. Press **Enter**. You can also type in Keywords, their Location by zip code, Title, Company, School they attended, their Industry or LinkedIn Groups they belong to, Language they speak, and how you want to sort the results. Then press **Enter**.

   The easiest way is to simply type their first and last names. When you get the search results, you'll see additional boxes to fill in on the right of your screen. When might you use these boxes?

   If the name is a common one like John Smith, you may get a huge number of matches. For example, when I looked up "John Smith" today, 12,701 users matched my search. It's daunting, if not impossible to look through that list to find the right John Smith. You can also Refine your Search Results by clicking on the box to the right on your results list. For example, simply add John Smith's Company and Location (country and zip code), and your search results list will be smaller and easier to manage.

The **Advanced Search** where you fill in a number of fields, is good when the person has a common name, or if you're looking for something like all of the Sales Vice Presidents in the Information Technology Services in New York. Click on *People* at the left top of the Home page. You'll see the Advanced Search area. Fill in appropriate Keywords, their Name, Title and Company. Choose from the lists for Location (country and zip code), Industry, what they're Interested in (potential employees, consultants/contractors, hiring managers, industry experts, etc.), when they joined your network, and how to sort your list of results. Then click *Search* and your list of matches comes up.

For Titles and Companies, you can check the box to search for current titles, past titles, current companies, past companies, or both current and past titles and companies. The search will only look at the section of the Profile where the current title and company are listed. It won't search through past titles and positions.

2. You can also do a **Reference Search** to get more information about potential employees, employers, and business partners. With this search, you'll find the people in your network who can provide professional references for your candidate. If the candidate is still with the company, enter 2009.

To do a Reference Search, click on *People* at the very top left of your screen. When you see the Advanced Search boxes, look for the tab with the word Reference in blue. Click on that tab, and you'll start your Reference search. This search gives you more information about potential employees, employers, and business partners.

- Enter the company names and the years the person worked at each company here. Your search will find the people in your network who can provide professional references for your candidate.
- If the candidate is still with the company, enter 2009. LinkedIn also gives you more search tips (near the bottom of this screen in blue.)

Refer to the screen shot for People searches on the next pages.

People Searches

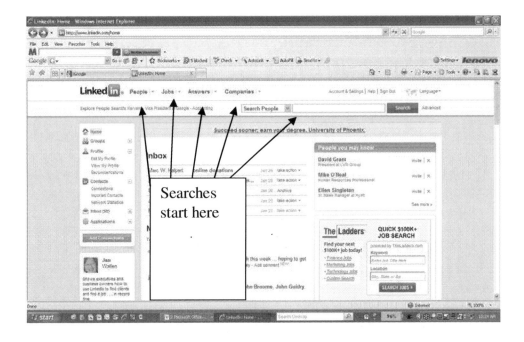

Start a People search: You'll see this after you click on People at the very top left of the Home page to do a search. Note the Advanced Search area below Name Search. To search for people in a geographic area, fill in the Postal Code. To do a Reference Search, click on the light green bar at the bottom of the screen.

People Searches

Start a People search here

Insider Tips for People Searches:

1. **Use Advanced Search fields right away to bring up a smaller results list.** That way it's more manageable, and you can easily find the specific person you're looking for.

2. **Be organized.** If you keep your contacts in ACT!, Excel or other contact manager, print out a list of your contacts, or contacts you're scheduled to be in touch with, and then go down the list to do your LinkedIn searches and connections or contacts.

3. When you use the search box at the top right of your screen, and you start typing a name, you'll see that LinkedIn finds people in your network whose name starts with what you're typing. LinkedIn **searches as you type**. Slide your mouse down and click on that person's name, and you'll go right to their LinkedIn Profile.

Action Steps for Tomorrow:

Do a real-life People search. For example, look for 5 people to connect with, 5 people who are in your industry, or perhaps a company whose business is similar to yours. See how they've written their LinkedIn Profiles, and get ideas for revising yours.

Name: _____

Name: _____

Name: _____

Name: _____

Name: _____

Search for Jobs

Login to LinkedIn and start at the LinkedIn Home page. Refer to the screen shot for Job searches later in this chapter.

1. **Search for a Job** on LinkedIn. Click on *Jobs* at the very top left of the screen. You'll see boxes to fill in Keywords, Country and Postal Code (zip code) with "Lookup" in blue to look up a zip code. Fill these in and click *Search* to get your list of results. Depending on the keywords you use here, it may take a few attempts before you get the results you want.

Start a Jobs Search – Jobs Home Screen on next page

Start a Jobs Search – Jobs Home Screen

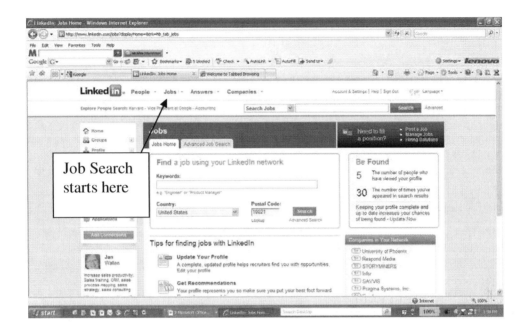

2. **Note the area** at the right side of the screen, "**Be Found**". This shows you the number of people who have viewed your Profile, and the number of times you've appeared in search results. Below that you see a list of the companies in your network.

3. At the bottom of the screen, you'll see "**Tips for finding jobs with LinkedIn**", and several things you can do to make it more likely that you'll find the position you're looking for and for recruiters to find you. For example, Update your Profile, Get Recommendations, and Add Connections. If you're seriously looking for a job, focus your time after you've completed this book on making good Connections and on getting Recommendations. Your Recommendations are ready references. And your Connections are the way you're more likely to get a new position than if you use the job boards.

4. To start your **Advanced Job Search**, start on the Advanced Jobs screen. Click on *Jobs* at the very top left of the screen. Then click the Advanced Job Search tab next to "Jobs Home". Fill in the appropriate search boxes

and click **Search**. For example, Job Title, Company, Job Function,
Industry and Experience Level.

Advanced Job Search Screen

Insider Tips for Job Searches:

1. **Be sure your LinkedIn Profile is up-to-date and puts your best
   face forward.** Expand descriptions and add keywords to your Profile
   so that it will be found easily by recruiters and hiring mangers.
   Carefully think through the keywords, including titles and
   responsibilities that the recruiters and hiring managers will be using in
   their searches. Be sure they're in your LinkedIn Profile.

2. **Be clear on exactly what you're looking for in your new position**,
   and make a list of potential companies that you want to work for.
   Know the titles of your decision-makers. That way your searches will
   pull up the best results, and you save time in your search.

3. **To find recruiters, do a People search on the keyword "recruiter".** Refine your search to include geographic areas, or specific companies.

4. **Do a Reference Search** to find people and companies where you worked and who could give you a reference. This is a good place for you to find people to ask for a Recommendation on LinkedIn. Let them know that you're looking and that they may be contacted for a reference. The hiring manager who may be considering you for a position may do a Reference Search and find the same people.

Action Steps for Tomorrow:

Do a real-life Job search for yourself. For example, look for 5 jobs using several different Keywords and titles or geographic areas.

Job and Keywords: _____

Job and Keywords: _____

Job and Keywords: _____

Job and Keywords: _____

Job and Keywords: _____

Search for Companies

When you search for Companies in LinkedIn, you'll find a tremendous amount of valuable information at your fingertips, and most of it is automatic. It doesn't depend on how well you construct your searches or how computer savvy you are about searches. LinkedIn has already thought through how business people will use these searches and the information they find.

The amount of information and the many possibilities for searches can be daunting. **Keep your searches to real-life situations** that will help you reach your goals and purpose for using LinkedIn. You'll see background for the company, number of employees, divisions, key statistics, who in your network works there, new hires, promotions and changes there, past employees, and news.

You may know someone you see here, or see someone you want to connect with. This is another way to make LinkedIn, which is so huge, more manageable. It brings people who are likely to be good connections directly to you.

Login to LinkedIn and start at the LinkedIn Home page. Refer to the screen shot for People searches above in this chapter.

1.   **Search for Companies** you know that are in LinkedIn. Make a list of companies you want to research or find people to connect with. Click on **Companies** at the very top left of the Home page. You'll see the boxes for Keywords, Country and Postal Code, and Industries below that. You can click on an industry there, or scroll down and you'll see "Browse all industries in blue. Click there to see all of the industries. Type in a Keyword, or type the specific Company name at the far right of the screen. Choose the country (or leave it as United States) and enter or look up the postal code and then click **Search**.

On the right of the screen there's a column to find a company by name, and below that you'll see the companies in your network. What's in that column changes depending on the specific search you do, and is very helpful in refining your searches to make it easier to find exactly what you're looking for.

As you start typing a Company name in the box on the right of the screen, a box with a listing of those companies and divisions comes up. Slide your mouse down to choose the one you want to review. Then you'll see a brief company description, which you can expand by clicking on **See more . . .** Look at the Company information in the center of the screen, and also in the right column.

You'll see your:
- Connections in that company,
- New Hires,
- Recent Promotions and Changes, and
- Popular Profiles.

In the right-hand column, you'll see Related Companies, Career Path for the Company's Employees, the Company's Employees most connected to . . ., and Key Statistics. This is very informative and good intelligence!

2. **Search for Industries.** Click on *Companies* at the very top left of the LinkedIn Home page. You'll see the boxes for Keywords, Country and Postal Code, and Industries below that. You can click on an industry there, or scroll down and you'll see "Browse all industries" in blue. Click there to see all of the industries. Choose the Industry you want to search from the list in the center of your screen, or click "Browse all industries" at the bottom of the list.

3. Then click on one of the industries. You'll see a list of companies in that industry. Scroll down to find the one(s) you're looking for and click on the company name to see more information.

4. On the right side of the screen, you'll see ways to modify and refine your search. This is especially good when your search results give you too many companies to manage or don't find exactly what you're looking for. For example, when I clicked on the industry Information Technology and Services today, 19,313 companies came up.

    When the companies list comes up, you'll see a blue box icon with a "1st" or "2nd" or "3rd" on the left next to each company name. That shows that you know someone at that company ("1st"), your connections know someone at that company ("2nd"), or someone who is connected to one of your connections knows someone at that company (3rd).

Start a Company Search on the next page

Company Search

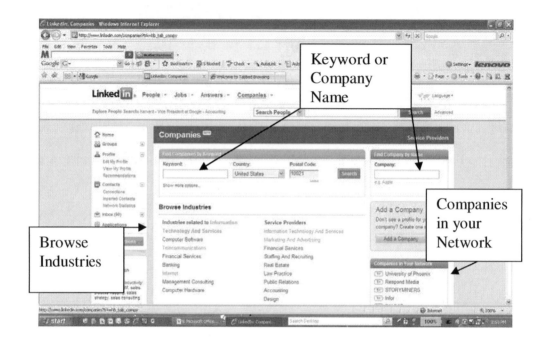

Insider Tips for Company Searches:

1. **Make a list of companies** you want to work for if you're looking for a job or potential clients if you're a sales manager, salespeople or a business owner building your business. When you find a company, look also at the career path for employees. You'll see companies that may also be appropriate for you to research further.

2. When you do a Company search, you also see New Hires and Recent Promotions and Changes. **Update your contact manager with the changes.** This is invaluable for updating your information.

3. **If you're changing careers or want to work or sell into a new area, contact people who are in that area and do some market research.** Ask them what it's like to work at that company or in that area. As a business owner, you can also do market research for new products and services you're developing. Call a potential decision-maker. Tell

them that you're developing new products and services, and ask them what their challenges are. Get their ideas on the products and services you're thinking about developing, and either go ahead, or refine them based on the information you get.

Action Steps for Tomorrow:

Do a real-life Company search. For example, look for 5 people to connect with or 5 people who are in your industry, or perhaps a company whose business is similar to yours. See how they've written their LinkedIn Profiles. Find your counterpart in these companies or your decision-maker if you're in sales or a business owner.

Company: _____

Company: _____

Company: _____

Company: _____

Company: _____

Search for Answers

The Answers section of LinkedIn is the area to **establish your Expert status** in your field and **build your company brand** and **visibility.** It's also a place to gather information that will help you in achieving our goals, in building your business and collaborating with people.

When you ask questions in LinkedIn Answers, the answers you get are from a more trusted network than a search engine or from unknown people on the Internet.

You can ask questions yourself and you can also look at and answer questions that other people have asked to get the information you're looking for. For example, when you click on Answers at the top of the LinkedIn Home screen, you'll see "New Questions from your Network" and "This Week's Top Experts".

Before you ask a question, look at the questions that others have asked to see if anyone else has already asked the same thing. Then if the answer you're looking for is not there, ask your question. Go to *Advanced Answers Search* first. Enter keywords and categories to see what questions have already been asked in the area of the question you want to ask. (See steps below)

Login to LinkedIn and start at the LinkedIn Home page. Refer to the screen shot for People searches later in this chapter.

1. **Search for Answers** on LinkedIn. Click on *Answers* at the left top of the Home page. You'll see the Answers screen with many things to look at. Scan them briefly, and take more time to explore each of them after you've browsed questions that other people have asked. Across the top you'll see:
    *   Answers Home
    *   Advanced Answers Search – go here first
    *   My Q&A
    *   Ask a Question, and
    *   Answer a Question

    Go to *Advanced Answers Search* first. Enter keywords and categories to see what questions have already been asked in the area of the question you want to ask.

    Below the top, you'll see:

    Ask a Question. Wait on this until you've browsed questions that other people have asked (below).

    Answer Questions. You'll do this in a few minutes, after you've browsed other questions and answers. Several categories of questions that you might want to answer have been suggested by LinkedIn

New Questions from your Network. Scroll down to review these. You'll also see who asked the question, where they are in your network (1st, 2nd or 3rd), how many answers there are, and how long ago they asked the question. You can review the question details by clicking on the blue underlined question, and click on the name of the person who asked the question to see their LinkedIn Profile.

This Week's Top Experts – people in your network who have answered the most questions in the past week

2. **Browse Questions** that have been asked before you ask your question. Click on *Browse* and then on a category for questions you want to view. You'll see who asked and answered questions, and category experts as you scroll down. You'll also see links to all the questions they've answered.

3. Take a few minutes to **explore the questions, categories, and experts** to get an idea of questions that have been asked and answered.

4. Write down the area(s) you want to **be known as the Expert** in. Choose categories from the lists you see in this section of LinkedIn. As you use LinkedIn more and more, devote time often to asking and especially to answering questions. This gives you visibility and the opportunity to build Expert status in your field.

5. Think of **5 questions you want to ask**, and list them and their categories.

6. Make a note of anyone you see here that you **want to connect with**. That's next.

7. **Ask a question**. Go back to the Answers Home screen (you'll see Answers Home at the top of the screen, or you can click on Answers at the top left). Click *inside the orange box "Ask a Question"* at the left of the screen, and type in your question. Be concise and clear. Then click *Next.* You move to a screen with your question at the top, and a box to check if you want to share this question only with connections that you select. For now, leave the box unchecked so that you get answers from the widest group of people. Add details if you want to clarify your question or what you're looking for in the answer, why you

want the answer, what you'll do with the information, etc. Select a category, and check the box if it's for a specific geographic location. And answer the questions at the bottom about your question being related to:

- Recruiting
- Promoting your services, or
- Job seeking

When you click **Ask Question**, your question will be displayed for people to *answer*.

Refer to the screen shot for Answers searches on the next pages.

Browse questions that have already been asked before you ask a question.

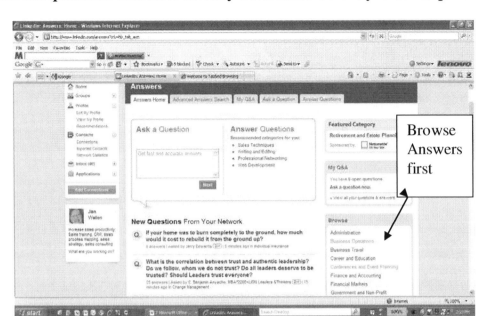

Insider Tips for Answers:

1. **Review your notes from the chapter on the Night Before** section in this book. Keep in mind the area you want to be known as an Expert in.

2. **Make a list of questions and types of Answers that will show your expertise in the area you want to be known for.** For example, when people see that you answer questions knowledgably about Public Relations, they will start to see you as an Expert in PR. And when they see that you've answered many questions, they'll also see you as an Expert.

3. **Set a goal for yourself to be known as the Expert**, and put a **timeline** on it. Remember, a goal without a timeframe is a wish.

4. **Every week or more frequently, look at the Answers and questions in that area. Participate by answering questions** and also asking them. You can gain Expertise points when your Answers are selected as the best Answers.

Action Steps for Tomorrow:

Make a list of 5-10 People to connect with. Be sure to include colleagues, classmates, and people in professional organizations and people you know now or want to know. You'll connect with people tomorrow who fit with your own situation and goals.

- _____

- _____

- _____

- _____

- _____

- _____

- _____

- _____

- _____

- _____

Day 3 – Connect

15-20 minutes

DAY 3 – Connect – 15-20 minutes

Your LinkedIn Profile is the cornerstone of your presence on LinkedIn, and how likely people are to do business with you or hire you. It's what people see when they do a search. They also see your Profile when you answer questions in the Answers section and when you write Recommendations for other people. And it's like your own personal Web site.

Here's an extra **Insider Secret** for you: **Always include this link to your LinkedIn Profile in your e-mail signature!** Your LinkedIn Profile is like your own personal Web page. Send people to it. And make it easy for them to click through to your LinkedIn Profile.

And put it as part of your **resume contact information**, the same as you put your phone number and e-mail address.

The link that LinkedIn automatically creates looks something like this: www.linkedin/in/468406ab. And that's exactly why you want to personalize it. People can't read this and see who you are. Personalizing your link so people see your name is one of the first steps for today.

Go to LinkedIn and log in. Look briefly at the names on the right side of the screen under **"People You May Know"**. The names that appear here are based on information in Profiles, and some will be people you know, and some will not. LinkedIn brings these names up automatically for you. You can see their Profiles (click on their names in blue) and to invite them to your network. Invitations will be covered in a later section of this book, and there's important information to know before you invite someone to be a part of your network, so for now, simply look. **Make it a habit of looking at these names whenever you login to LinkedIn.** You'll connect with people you may never have thought of or known about. An interesting thing that's happened several times to me is that "Jan Wallen" comes up on that list as people I may know (!)

Step 1 – Review and Add to your Profile, and Check your Contact Settings

Login to LinkedIn and start at the LinkedIn Home page.

1. **Review your LinkedIn Profile and ask yourself:** Does it help me reach my goals and my purpose for being on LinkedIn? Is my Profile compelling and up-to-date? If you searched and found your Profile, would *I* pick up the phone to call right away to hire me or do business with me?

2. **Add or change** things you thought of since yesterday, and from ideas you got from seeing other peoples' Profiles.

3. Add your **photo** if you haven't already done that. When people see a Profile without a photo, they skip right over it, and go to someone else's Profile. Put a photo up, even if it's not perfect.

4. **Make a list of people you will request Recommendations from**. These are like references, only more specific, and a very important factor in people hiring or doing business with you. List the people you'll write Recommendations for.

5. **Review your list of questions you want to ask** in the Answers section of LinkedIn, and add to it.

6. **Double-check** to be sure your Profile gets across what you want it to when people see it. Make notes for further revisions. Especially when you're creating your Profile for the first time, you'll be adding to it and changing it frequently. And you'll continue to add to it and change it as your goals change and you get a new position or clients, offer new services, etc.

   You'll be answering questions soon in the Answers section. Your answers include a link to your Profile, so you want your Profile to be complete and optimized as much as possible. When people read your Profile, they're very likely to click on the link to your Profile, so you want it to accurately reflect who you are. Your Profile should be finished for now. Review your Profile periodically and update it to accurately show your activities and expertise.

7. **Look at your Contact Settings.** At the bottom of your Profile when you View your Profile, you'll see your Contact Settings – ones you've selected when you created your Profile. For example, consulting ventures, job inquiries, business deals, getting back in touch, etc. Below that you'll see a box about your Contact Settings, and a way to change those settings.

For example, it says:

"How a user can contact you depends on how he or she is connected to you:

- If a connection views your profile, he or she sees your e-mail address

- If a user in your network views your profile, he or she sees a "Get Introduced" button

- If a user in the LinkedIn network tries to view your profile, he or she will see an anonymous profile and a "Contact Directly" button."

- And you can click on "Change your contact settings" in blue to change your settings. Click there and you'll go to the Account & Settings section, and your Contact Settings. Check the boxes that you want for how people see your profile. Remember, if you're looking for a job, you want most people to see all of your profile. You may not always want that, and can change it later when your situation and goals change. Note: You can also change these settings from your LinkedIn Profile. Click on "Edit Public Profile Settings" in the top right corner of the screen.

Step 2 – Personalize the Link to your LinkedIn Profile, so people know it's you – i.e., your Vanity URL

Login to LinkedIn and start at the LinkedIn Home page. Refer to the screen shot for People searches on the next pages.

1. **Go to your Profile Home page** (Click on *Profile* at the top left corner of the LinkedIn Home page). You'll see your Profile. Scroll down part way down and look in the center of the screen, after:
   1. Current
   2. Past
   3. Education
   4. Recommended
   5. Connections
   6. Web sites

   At the bottom of this boxed-in area, you'll see "**Public Profile**" at the bottom of the boxed area, with the link to your Profile.

   (**NOTE**: Your list may look different, depending on whether your settings permit people to see all of these or if you've filled them out in your Profile.)

2. **Note the link.** It will look something like www.linkedin.com/in/468406/0/376/b. That's the link that LinkedIn gives you automatically.

3. **Now personalize your link** so it's easy to read and people know it's you.

   At the end of your link, you'll see [Edit] in blue. Click on *[Edit]*.

   (If you don't see [Edit], you may see [Hide]. Click on [Hide] and you should see [Edit].)

   You go to a new page, and you'll see **"Your Public Profile URL" and your URL** at the top of the screen. For example, it will look something like: www.linkedin.com/in/468406/0/376/b.

   Next to "Your Public Profile URL" is your link, and at the right you'll see [Edit]. Click on *[Edit]*.

   (If you don't see [Edit], you may see [Hide]. Click on [Hide] and you should see [Edit].)

You'll go to a new page again, and you'll see "Your Public Profile URL", information about it, and a white box where you personalize the link to your LinkedIn Profile.

** *IMPORTANT* **

In that box, **type your full name** in all lower case letters, and as one word. Then click *Set Address*. That changes the link from the unreadable numbers and letters to your name. For example, after I personalized the link to my Profile, it says:
www.linkedin.com/in/janwallen.

4. **Now that your link is personalized, use it!** Put it in your e-mail signature the same way that you put your company name, e-mail address, phone number and Web site. Put it on your resume with your contact information. People I would not have found or known about have clicked through to my Profile after they saw the link in my e-mail signature, and invited me to connect. I like to make it stand out and make it clear to people what it is, so in my e-mail signature, I put:

Jan Wallen
LinkedIn Works!
www.LinkedInWorks.com
(877) 327-5058
My LinkedIn Profile: www.linkedin.com/in/janwallen

Edit the link to your Public Profile: On your Profile page, click on Edit. See next page.

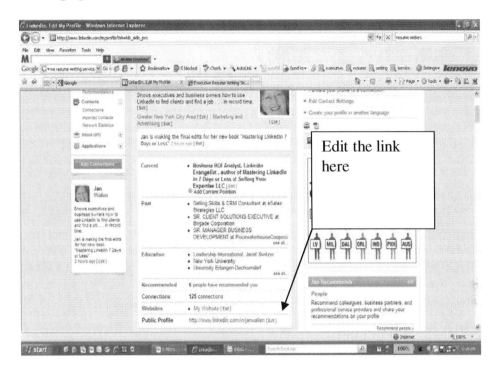

You've now created your LinkedIn Profile, and you've personalized the link to your public profile so that people know it's you. **Use it as part of your e-mail signature from now on, so they'll check out your profile.** Your LinkedIn Profile is like your own personal Web page.

You also know the basics of searching for people and companies.

Having your LinkedIn Profile up is critical in inviting people to connect, especially for people who don't yet know you. That's how they'll make the decision to connect and network with you or not.

So . . . the next step is to Connect and send invitations out.

Step 3 – Connect

Think about your network and how you want to build it. Your overall goal is to build a network of people who you know, like and trust. And who have mutual interests, experience, connections, and who also believe in networking. You want to connect with them on a regular basis. Online networking is similar to in-person networking in that way.

Decision Point: **You may or may not want to connect with everyone you know or correspond with.** There are two philosophies for building your network: Building a Quality network or building a Quantity network. These work for both online and in-person networking. The Quality philosophy is where you know everyone in your network personally or at least by a conversation with them, and you don't invite everyone or accept anyone's invitation to join. The Quantity philosophy is you want to connect with as many people as possible. This is also known in LinkedIn as being an Open Networker or LION.

1. If you've already connected with people, click on Contacts in the left column – the Home Base at the top -- and you'll see a **list of your Contacts**. You can also see Imported Contacts, and Network Statistics – your Connections, and people who are two degrees away and 3 degrees away. (LinkedIn is based on the 6 degrees of separation.) You can add Connections by looking at and importing your Outlook contacts or your contacts from a webmail service like Yahoo Mail, Hotmail or Gmail, or invite people one at a time. For now, invite one person you already know to connect and be a part of your network.

2. To **add a Contact now**, go to Contacts – Click on *Contacts* on the left top of the Home page. Click on *Add Connections* at the top right of the screen. Fill in the first name, last name and e-mail address of someone you want to connect with. *IMPORTANT*: Click on *Preview invitation text*! LinkedIn automatically gives you an invitation message that is handy; however, it's really bland and unfriendly. Always **personalize it** before you send the invitation. Add a friendly "Hello!" and something about why you want to connect. If it's someone you already know, your personal message may be shorter than for someone you don't yet know.

3. Click on *Send Invitation(s)*. LinkedIn adds a link for them to click to accept your invitation and an explanation about invitations. When your contact sees your invitation, they have several choices. They can:

Accept – They accept your invitation and become part of your network. When they accept, LinkedIn sends you an e-mail called LinkedIn Connections, and when you open the e-mail, you go to their acceptance notice. You can look at their Profile, download it, and continue building your network. You can also write a Recommendation for them. I highly recommend doing this because Recommendations are such an important part of LinkedIn.

Archive – If you get an invitation and don't want to accept it, you can archive it without responding.

Reply – If you're not sure if you want to accept an invitation, you can send the person a message to find out how they found you and how they see you networking together. Look for the small word *Reply* at the bottom right of your screen. You can reply and send a message to them before you decide to accept their invitation. Click on *Reply* to send a message.

I don't know this user – This has implications in LinkedIn beyond the words. Part of the LinkedIn philosophy is that people connect with people they know, and that spamming or connecting outside the Terms of Service is not acceptable. If 5 people respond to a person who has invited them, and uses "I don't know this person", that person's account can be terminated from LinkedIn. Don't use this. Take time to look at their Profile and contact them about how they see that you can network together. Then if it makes sense, connect. Otherwise, archive it.

To find out what to do when you get an invitation from someone you don't know, see Insider Secret #2 below.

Realistically, in a community like LinkedIn, you're there to network, and you'll be networking with people you don't know yet. For example, you don't yet know the next person who will hire you or who will be your next client until you make the connection and start to build a relationship.

Even if you decide to not connect, *don't* use "I don't know NAME". Simply Archive it.

Insider Secrets:

1. Here's an *Insider Secret that works every time*: In your invitation, always ask the person how you can help them or ask what you can do for them. One thing you can do if you know them or have worked with them is to offer to write a Recommendation. In LinkedIn, Recommendations are like ready references, and are very helpful to people in completing their Profiles and to accomplish whatever they want to do because anyone who finds them in a search looks at their Recommendations.

2. **If you get an invitation from someone you don't know, don't immediately Archive it. Take time to look at their Profile**, see what you have in common and if they seem to be a good connection. Then contact them – either Reply to their invitation (you'll see where to do that when you get the invitation) and say you're interested in knowing them better. Ask how they found you, and what they saw in your LinkedIn Profile that attracted or interested them. Or pick up the phone and talk to them. After your phone conversation, decide if you want to accept their invitation or not. I've met wonderful connections that way. And even if you decide to not connect, *don't* use "I don't know NAME". Simply Archive the invitation.

3. **Think about your network and how you want to build it.** Your overall goal is to build a network of people you know, like and trust, and who have mutual interests, experience, connections; who also believe in networking. And to connect with them on a regular basis. Online networking is similar to in-person networking in that way.

4. **A fast, easy way to add people to your network** is to look at the names on the Home page at the right of the screen, "People you May Know". Look for people you know, and click on their name there. When you click on their name, you'll see their Profile, and be able to:
   - Send InMail
   - Get introduced by a colleague
   - Add them to your network, and
   - Forward this profile to a connection

   Remember to personalize the invitation with a friendly message that reminds them of how you know them.

Success Stories:

A situation that came up for me recently shows the power of LinkedIn. I'm a member of MENG (Marketing Executives Networking Group), a networking organization of senior sales and marketing executives. It's also a Group in LinkedIn. We have a forum where we can ask questions of the other MENG members. For example, we can request referrals for services that a client is looking for, or opinions, thoughts and ideas from members who have had experience in an area that's relevant to what we're working on. I posted a request, and a day or so later, I received an e-mail saying that a fellow MENG member wanted to connect with me on LinkedIn. His message explained that he'd seen my post on the MENG forum with the link to my LinkedIn Profile in my e-mail signature. That prompted him to look at my LinkedIn Profile. Which prompted him to contact me via LinkedIn and connect. We've now connected, and had a good phone meeting and introduction. We've each offered to help the other one with our goals, and continue to network. We may even meet at some point in the future, because we both travel.

Action Steps for Tomorrow:

Think of people you've worked with, in professional organizations, events where you worked together, your clients and alumni of your university or college. Make a list and jot notes down of their strengths, and the projects or ways that you worked together.   Tomorrow you'll start writing Recommendations for them.

1. _____

2. _____

3. _____

4. _____

5. _____

6. _____

7. _____

8. _____

9. _____

10. _____

Day 4 – Recommendations

15-20 minutes

DAY 4 –Write a Recommendation for a Colleague – 15-20 minutes

Recommendations are real gems in LinkedIn. They are ready references that people who've worked with you write for you, and you write for them. For example, you'll want to get Recommendations from colleagues from companies where you've worked before, from school and people who know you now or have worked with you as a consultant.

The way they're written is important. People who look at your Profile will also look at your Recommendations, so be sure they're relevant to:
- the work you've done together
- your expertise
- your strengths
- responsibilities you've had, and
- characteristics and qualities that show you in a good light. For example, show your initiative, problem-solving abilities, and mini-case stories or success stories.

If someone writes a Recommendation for you and it's doesn't show these things or isn't to your satisfaction, ask them to revise it OR, better yet, revise it and send it back to them and ask them if the new version works for them. If so, ask them to add anything else that's relevant or revise it. People are usually glad to do that.

An excellent way to get started with a new connection is to offer to write a Recommendation for them. See the Insider Secrets below for tips and proven strategies, and take a look at Recommendations on other peoples' Profiles to see how they're written.

No matter what you want to do on LinkedIn, having Recommendations is the second most important thing on LinkedIn, next to having your Profile up. You can't do anything in LinkedIn without your Profile. While you can technically do things on LinkedIn without having Recommendations, you won't go as far as fast. Recommendations are ready references. People who are looking for their next superstar employee or the company they want to hire look at the Profile first, and also at the Recommendations before deciding whether to connect or not. When a client is looking for a company or consultant to work with, they want to see Recommendations, too.

It may be helpful as you write your first Recommendations to look at Recommendations that have been written for other LinkedIn members. You can search for people you know, look at the Profiles for the people you see on the Home page on the right side of the screen (People You May Know), or LinkedIn Updates as you scroll down the screen. And look at Profiles for your counterparts at other companies. Remember that you're giving someone a reference that will be read by many people for various purposes. Make it relevant and be sure you show the person and their expertise in a strong positive light.

Step 1 – Find a Colleague and Write a Recommendation for Them

Login to LinkedIn and start at the LinkedIn Home page. Refer to the screen shots for Recommendations later in this chapter.

1. **Search for a colleague** you want to write a Recommendation for. Do a People search. Click on *People* at the top of the screen, and fill in their first and last names. Use Advanced Search fields if they have a common name and your search results will give you a list of too many names to look through to find the right one. For example, if you're looking for "John Smith", use the Advanced Search fields and fill in his company and/or geographic area. When I searched for "John Smith" today, there were 12,977 John Smiths.

2. **Go to their Profile.** Look to the right of the screen, and you'll see **Recommend this person**. Click there, and you'll see where you can manage Recommendations you've sent. Scroll down, and you'll see **Make a Recommendation**.

3. Enter their name and e-mail address (or select it from your connections list – click there). Select how you know the person – Colleague, Service Provider, Business Partner, Student – then click *Continue*. If you select Service Provider, their company and your Recommendation will go into the Service Provider directory of LinkedIn. *Select Service Provider when you recommend a client or service provider you've*

hired, even if you also know them as a Colleague or Business Partner. It spotlights them, and people who are looking for service providers will find them.

4. **Fill in** the boxes that appear, making your selection from the drop-down boxes: Position, Service Category, and Year first hired. Choose their Top Attributes. When you choose these, keep in mind that people who find this person's Profile will decide whether to connect with or hire this person and their company based in part on your Recommendation. Choose the attributes that both reflect those that you found when you worked with them, *and also those that will help other people make the decision to hire them*.

Write a Recommendation

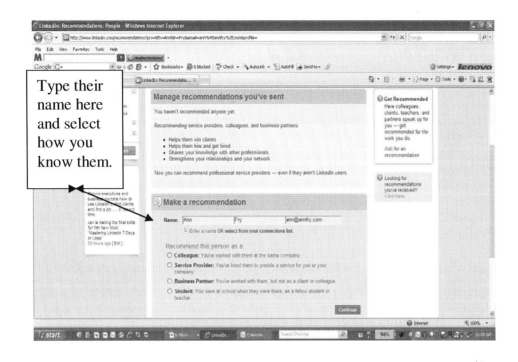

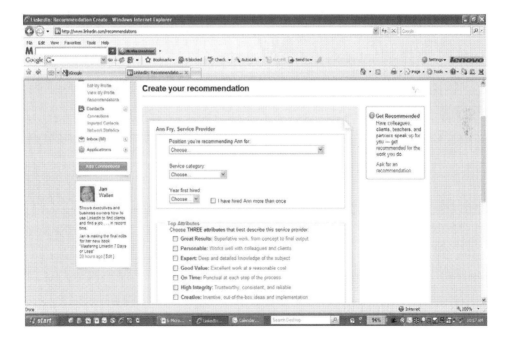

Step 2 – Write your Recommendation

1. **Write your Recommendation** in the box provided. Be sure it's specific and results-oriented, so the person reading it can't wait to connect with and hire that person and their company. When you've written your Recommendation, a message will be sent to your colleague with your Recommendation. It's a handy, though rather bland message: "I've written this recommendation of your work to share with other LinkedIn users." Personalize it, as you have the Invitation message, and make it friendly. After all, you know them well enough to write this Recommendation!

2. **Review** several Recommendations before you write yours. Find Recommendations that you like, and use them as examples.

3. **A time-saving way** to write a Recommendation is to contact your colleague and tell them that you want to write a Recommendation for them. Ask them what will be helpful to them. For example, what areas of their expertise, strengths, responsibilities and qualities or characteristics they want to have you mention. You can also draft the Recommendation and send it to them before you write in on LinkedIn. If they have any revisions, they'll send them to you, and it will be a lot easier to write their Recommendation once you're in LinkedIn.

Step 3 – Finalizing your Recommendation

The person you write a Recommendation for can **review it and accept it**, or ask that you revise it. If they accept it, then they add it to their Profile. When someone writes a Recommendation for you, take time to review it, and ask them to revise it if it doesn't reflect what you want it to reflect. It's helpful to them if you outline several things to include, or tell them that you're looking for a position or new clients, and want their Recommendation to mention things that are relevant to that.

You can also **Request a Recommendation** from colleagues who have worked with you. Make it a habit to request Recommendations every week. These are ready references from people who are satisfied with you and your work. It also puts you in the Service Providers directory (if that's appropriate for you). Also make it a habit to offer to write a Recommendation when you connect with a colleague. Many times they will offer to write one for you in return.

Go to **Recommendations** in the box on the far left side of the screen (from anywhere in LinkedIn). You'll see 3 tabs in the blue box:

- Received Recommendations
- Sent Recommendations
- Request Recommendations

Click on *Request Recommendations* and fill in the boxes. They're self-explanatory. Personalize the request message that LinkedIn gives you, and then send it off to your colleague.

When someone writes a Recommendation for you, you choose whether to show it on your LinkedIn Profile or not. You can change the ones that show to be most appropriate for your goals, or so people see different ones over time.

Insider Secrets:

1. **The way Recommendations are written is important.** People who look at your Profile will also look at your Recommendations and decide whether to connect with you, to hire you, work with you, or refer you to someone else. Be sure they're relevant to:
   - the work you've done together
   - your expertise
   - your strengths
   - responsibilities you've had, and
   - characteristics and qualities that show you in a good light. For example, show your initiative, problem-solving abilities,

2. **Use keywords in your Recommendations.** Completed LinkedIn Profiles are found by search engines.

3. **Writing a Recommendation for someone also puts your Profile on display too.** In real estate, it's "Location, Location, Location". In marketing and LinkedIn, it's "Frequency, Frequency, Frequency"!!!

Draft the Recommendation you want to write and send it to your colleague for his or her review and revisions *before* you post it on LinkedIn. When they send it back to you with any revisions, it will be easy to put it in LinkedIn.

Action Steps for tomorrow:

1. **Review your LinkedIn Profile. As you connect with people and look at their Profiles, you may see ways to change yours. If you have extra time today, make those changes. If not, jot notes down of the changes that you want to make.**

   - _____

   - _____

   - _____

   - _____

   - _____

   The Answers section of LinkedIn is where you can get answers to questions that will help you with your work, for your professional development, and to establish your status as an Expert in your field.

2. **Write down 3-5 things that you want to be known as the Expert for.** You may be like many of my clients, who are multi-talented, with many things that you *can* do. Pick *one* to be known for. You can't be an Expert at everything. For example, when you think of golf experts, who do you think of? Tiger Woods. What's your area?

If you're not sure, write down several that you think of, think about it for the next week, and then pick one. If you're still not sure, send an e-mail to me at info@linkedinworks.com and put What's My Expertise? in the Subject line or call me at (877) 327-5058. We'll set a time to talk and you'll know exactly what your real expertise is.

- _____
- _____
- _____
- _____
- _____

3. **Write down 5 questions you'll ask your LinkedIn network.**

- _____
- _____
- _____
- _____
- _____

Day 5 – Answers
15-20 minutes

DAY 5 – Answers – 15-20 minutes

LinkedIn gives us a place to connect and network, and also to share our expertise, ask questions and get answers. In fact the answers are from fellow business people rather than the entire Internet where you don't really know the quality of the information. People are asking questions about things they want to know that will help them with their careers or businesses, and things that their clients want to know. LinkedIn stores the questions and answers, as well as who asked and answered them for everyone to refer to. It's a wonderful repository of information, and right at our fingertips.

With the Answers section of LinkedIn, you can:
- Build your brand and visibility
- Ask questions about people or your connections
- Ask questions that will help get your work done
- Ask questions related to personal and professional development
- Build your status as an Expert in your area

Step 1 – Browse to See if Someone has Already Asked your Question

Login to LinkedIn and start at the LinkedIn Home page. Refer to the screen shot for Answers later in this chapter.

1. **Think of questions to ask and make a list. Keep it handy** in your LinkedIn folder or in a document, so it's easy to go to LinkedIn and ask them.

2. Look to **see if the question has been asked before**, and to get ideas of questions you want to ask. To browse questions that have been asked, look at the categories under Browse, on the right side of the screen. **Click on the category** that's closest to the topic of your question to see the questions that people have asked. Categories include:
   - Administration
   - Business Operations
   - Career and Education

- Finance and Accounting
- Financial Markets
- Government and Non-Profit
- Hiring and Human Resources
- International
- Law and Legal
- Management
- Marketing and Sales
- Personal Finance
- Product Management
- Startups and Small Businesses
- Technology
- Using LinkedIn

As an example, a category I always check is Marketing and Sales, since my expertise is in sales, networking and building relationships. The Marketing and Sales questions from my network are in the center of the screen. Within that category, there are sub-categories, and you'll see them on the right:
- Advertising and Promotion
- Business Development
- Graphic Design
- Mobile Marketing
- Public Relations
- Sales
- Search Marketing
- Writing and Editing

3. **Browse the one that's closest to your topic.** Click the *category name*, and scroll down to see the questions. Then click the title of the question to see the details. You'll see the person who asked the question, and below their name, you can click on "See all my answers" to see the questions they've answered. You can go to their Profile, and when you scroll down, you'll see the answers to their question.

4. Below the category heading you'll see "Open Questions" and "Closed Questions". **Check them both** to see if your question has been asked. For Open questions, the person who asked is still accepting answers. For Closed questions, the person who asked them is no longer accepting answers.

5. **Check out the answers by "This Week's Top Experts"** – scroll down your screen until you see their names. When you ask a question in a category and in a LinkedIn public forum, the person who asked the question can pick your answer as the best answer. LinkedIn then gives you a point. When you answer questions, you accumulate expertise points, *and* your visibility as an Expert. It's well worth it to answer questions and increase your visibility and credibility. It's a good way to build your brand.

6. If you don't see the question you want to ask, go to the top of the screen and click on *Advanced Answers Search*. Fill in the Keywords, Category and choose to see only the unanswered questions or not. Then click *Search*.

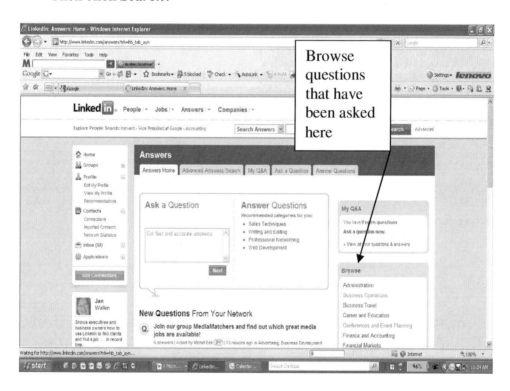

Step 2 – Ask your Question

1. When you've established that the question you want to ask hasn't been asked before, **ask your question** by clicking on *Ask Question*. You can also ask a question from the Answers Home page on the left by filling in the box that says, "Get answers from your connections and experts in your network."

2. From the Answers Home page or the pages where you were browsing, click on *Ask a Question*.

3. **Ask your question by filling in the boxes.** Check out the examples – click on *See examples* in blue. You can check the box to share this question with your connections that you select; however, you'll get fewer answers. Think of the first box as the headline for your question. Add details to clarify what you mean, why you're asking the question, or an example. Choose the category and geographic location if it's relevant. Answer the questions at the bottom:

    Is your question related to?
    1. Recruiting
    2. Promoting your services
    3. Job seeking

4. **Review the answers, and perhaps respond to or connect with people who answered** your question.   Always look for good relationships to build.

Step 3 – Answer Questions

Answering questions increases your visibility and credibility, and is an excellent way to build your brand. Devote time to Answers regularly and consistently to stay on the radar screen.

1. Start at the Answers Home page. Click on *Answer Questions* (in small blue print at the top right of the screen). **NOTE:** There's more than one way to answer questions in LinkedIn. For now, use the way I'll describe. Otherwise you'll miss important things.
2. Now you can now **Browse Open Questions**, or Browse by category from the list on the right.

3. **Look for questions where your answer will highlight your expertise**, and where it may be selected as the best answer. This way, you're more focused, and you'll establish your status as an Expert, as well as increasing your visibility and credibility.

4. When you find a question you want to answer, **click on the question to answer it.** You'll see the question at the top, and the person who asked it. You can view their Profile if you want to. To answer the question, click on the Answer box. To suggest an Expert, click on the Suggest the Expert box. You have the option of answering privately or your answer will be seen by all LinkedIn users. If there are Web resources that support your answer, you can list them. You can also suggest an Expert and write a note to the person who asked the question if you want to. When you've answered and are ready to submit your answer, click *Submit*.

Insider Secrets:

1. **Browsing the questions also shows you other people who are in your industry or related area.** You may want to connect and collaborate with them. They could be joint venture partners, or you may create strategic alliances, or collaborate on projects.

2. **When you answer questions, you accumulate expertise points, *and* visibility as an Expert**. It's well worth it to answer questions and increase your visibility and credibility. It's a good way to build your brand.

3. **When you have the opportunity, highlight your clients in your Answers.** For example, if someone is looking for ways to fund a documentary film, and one of your clients does that, answer the question and tell them about your client. Your clients will love you for promoting them!

4. **Earning Expertise Points**

    When you see this star on a profile, you know that person has proven their expertise by answering questions.

    Earning Expertise is easy. LinkedIn describes how to do it this way in the LinkedIn "Help" section.

- ***Find questions in the areas you know***
  Browse questions to find categories familiar to you
- ***Answer those questions***
  Remember, private answers won't help you earn expertise
- ***Every time the questioner picks your answer best, you gain a point of expertise***
  The more points of expertise, the higher you appear on lists of experts

Action Steps for Tomorrow:

Tomorrow you'll start using what you've learned so far, and apply it to your own specific situation and goals. You'll review your Profile, connect with people, write and ask for Recommendations, and do searches so you can start doing this quickly. Being successful in networking and with LinkedIn is possible with 15-20 minutes a day.

So think of real People, Jobs or Companies you want to connect with, search for, request and write Recommendations for, and in a word "Network" with. Review your goals from the *Night Before Day 1* chapter to be sure you're on track. Write your notes here.

Day 6 – Power Up LinkedIn & Turn Up the Speed

15-20 minutes

DAY 6 – Power Up LinkedIn & Turn Up the Speed – 15-20 minutes

In your first 5 days, you've joined LinkedIn if you weren't a member already, found people you know, people you want to know, job listings and companies of interest. You've also invited people to connect and be a part of your network, and most likely accepted invitations from people you know. And you've written and requested Recommendations or ready-references.

So you know the basics of using LinkedIn. Now is the time to power it up, and really use it for networking. You'll do that today.

Before you start today, review your goals and purpose for using LinkedIn from the *Night Before Day 1* chapter. Your purpose and goals may or may not be the same as they were when you started reading this book. For example, if you were looking for a job, that may still be your overall purpose. And now that you know LinkedIn better and see what a powerful tool it is, you may have a better idea of strategies that you'll use to reach your goals. It may also be helpful to review the chapters in the book. Ask yourself these questions:

1. Now that you know LinkedIn more, **are your goals and purpose the same** as they were when you started a week ago? What are your goals now?

- Find a job – through recruiters being
- able to find me and networking people
- being easily able to contact me for a job lead
- Reconnect on a personal level with the people I worked with in the past

2. What are the **Top 3 strategies** you'll use in networking with LinkedIn? For example, what time of day will you devote to your networking? And how much time each week? Will you search for new people and connect with them, or network more with people who are already in your network? There's no one right answer here – the best way is the way that fits you.

- List/find all people I currently know.
- After identifying target companies, find people
- through my network in those companies. Ask for introduction.

3. What will **be most helpful to learn** more about and devote more time to? Will Advanced Searches be helpful to know? Or focus on updating your LinkedIn Profile?

- Get profile to be compelling w/Jeb
- Ask Jan for review
- Look at profiles of all my contacts for ideas
- Jan more groups

4. Networking is a very effective way of marketing when you use it regularly, consistently and with a plan. What will your **networking "marketing plan"** be? Write your plan here:

1) Get my profile done
2) Research target companies
3) Share profile & how someone can help with all my contacts

5. **Who will you ask for Recommendations?** These are ready references, and are very important to people who find your LinkedIn Profile. All things being equal in terms of background and skills, the person with Recommendations has a higher perceived value.

- *Get Deb opinion on Recommendation. Decide*
- _____
- _____
- _____
- _____

6. **Who will you write Recommendations for?** This is a great way to reconnect with someone you've been out of touch with. Everyone wants Recommendations, and they really are helpful no matter what their goals are.

- *When reaching out to connect, have*
- *a recom strategy in mind*
- _____
- _____
- _____

Now it's time to power up LinkedIn and make it work for you.

Login to LinkedIn and start at the LinkedIn Home page.

Step 1 – The Most Important 10 Minutes You'll Ever Spend on LinkedIn

Start powering up LinkedIn by backing up your Contacts and Profile.

This is an article I wrote after I learned that someone's LinkedIn Profile was accidentally deleted from LinkedIn. ***Follow these steps ASAP***. If you know people who don't know about backing up your LinkedIn network, tell them right away. They can get a copy of the article by sending an e-mail to me at: info@linkedinworks.com and putting Back Up My LinkedIn in the Subject line.

You've spent a lot of time and given a lot of attention to your LinkedIn Profile. And when you're using LinkedIn to network and build your business, enhance your career with a new position, or find your next superstar employee, you have valuable information and connections at your fingertips.

It's come to my attention through a colleague and fellow LinkedIn connection that a LinkedIn member's account was accidentally deleted from LinkedIn. (My thanks to Jason Alba and Diane Mensinger for bringing this to my attention.) And that meant her Profile, Contact and Connections were lost. Yes, lost. All that time, effort and information – gone.

Yes, you can start over. Though it may not be easy unless you've kept the same information in your contact manager, taken good notes, and have an excellent memory. And have a lot of time.

Here's what you can do to be sure that information in your LinkedIn account is not lost, even accidentally. ***This is a must-do, ASAP!*** Don't wait until the end of the day or "tomorrow". It can be the most important 10 minutes you ever spend on LinkedIn. Do it ***now!***

1. **Export your Contacts.** Log in to LinkedIn and click on **Contacts**. Go down to the bottom of the screen and click on Export Connections. You'll see an icon of a grayed square with a green arrow pointing down. Follow the steps until your contacts are exported. Don't change any of the defaults – leave everything as it is. When you're finished, you'll have a .CSV file that you can open in Excel. (You can export your contacts in several formats. The easiest is the .CSV file. The default for this says,

"Microsoft Outlook".) After you export your contacts, you'll be able to see the instructions for importing your newly exported file to:

- o Microsoft Outlook
- o Outlook Express
- o Yahoo! Mail
- o Mac OS X Address Book"

You now have the **Contact information** for all of the people you've connected with, including their e-mail addresses. *WOW! A real loss if something happens!*

The **Recommendations** you've received are also captured here. These are priceless!

2. **Save your Profile.** Click on Profile, and look for the grayed out icons above your name. You'll see an icon for a printer, one for Adobe PDF, one for a vCard, and one to bookmark a Profile. Click on the Adobe PDF icon. A box appears. Choose "Save" (rather than "Open"). Select the directory where you want to save your Profile. Change the name of the file if you want to. The automatic format for mine is: jan_wallen.pdf. This saves your Profile to a PDF document that's formatted very nicely.

Your Call to Action:

Go *now* to LinkedIn and back up your priceless network. "Do not pass Go! Do not collect $200". Do it *now*!

See the screen shots below.

Backing Up your Profile and Contacts

Saving your LinkedIn Profile - On your Profile screen

Contacts screen – top. Scroll down to Export your Contacts.
Scroll down to the bottom to Export your Contacts.

Scroll down to the bottom to Export your Contacts. See the next page.

Export your Connections.

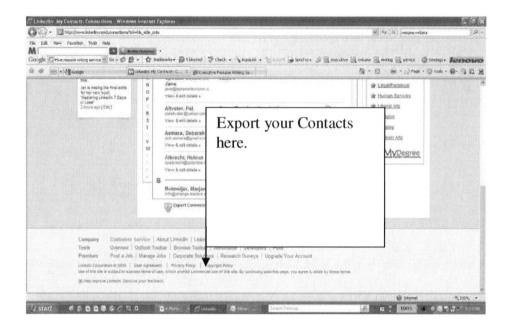

Export your Contacts here.

Step 2 – Ask for and Write Recommendations

1. **Write Recommendations for at least 5 colleagues.** Review Day 4 about how to write Recommendations. Do this enough that it's easy to both ask for them and write them.

2. **Ask for at least 5 Recommendations.** Make it easier for them to write it by giving the people you ask some specifics and reference points to include when they write it. Be sure it's results-oriented.

3. **Review the Recommendations you see when you look at LinkedIn Profiles.** Get ideas for how to write them for other people.

Step 3 – Build your Network and Connect

1. **Invite people to be a part of your network.** Take time to personalize your invitation message and really connect. Take time to look at:
   - People in your network
   - People in the networks of your connections
   - People You May Know (on the Home page)
   - Network Updates (on the Home page)
   - Groups and people in the groups

   Look at their Profiles and see if they'd be a good connection, or if they know someone else you know. This is a good way to start another connection and relationship. If both of you know the same person, pick up the phone and make the connection.

   Make it a habit to find things in common. These are excellent ice-breakers to start new business relationships.

2. **Be sure your Profile is up-to-date, has the appropriate keywords, and fits your current goals and purpose on LinkedIn.**

Success Story:

This Success Story is from a colleague who was starting a job search. Here's what she said:

"Recently I was part of a major downsizing that took my entire department and left me jobless for the first time in my life. I met Jan Wallen through a friend a few months before, and we had networked via email and attempted (and failed) phone conversations. It was amazing how quickly Jan offered to walk beside me and be my LinkedIn Coach when she heard my bad news. Now, I am old enough that some online things create a challenge for me. When I first got invited to connect on LinkedIn my thought was, "This is nice...a good way to keep my contact information." Never, never did I realize the functionality and power of LinkedIn until Jan spent coaching time with me.

In her first hour session I learned the power of putting a link to my personal Profile in my signature line of my email, the importance of completing my Profile, of changing my Profile often so new keywords are used and picked up, of joining groups and using those networks to increase my reach. Just this morning I received a note from a sorority sister who lives in Jacksonville asking me for my resume.

The second coaching session was focused on job searches and how the network really reaches to others. I had an incredible experience when I found someone in my 3rd level (an executive with a grocery store chain headquartered locally), was connected to a person in my first level. I asked for an introduction and have now been in contact with the grocery store executive. It dawned on me then that this is the beauty of LinkedIn and what Jan has been sharing with me. After a week of really using the tool I am just realizing how effective this online network can be. The best reminder is knowing that people want to be found on LinkedIn and that is why they are there. This is an incredible tool for meeting people and advancing professional goals and knowledge. Thank you, Jan Wallen, for wakening my senses and putting me in contact with some really wonderful people."

Insider Secrets:

1. **Stay on track.** Write your LinkedIn purpose and goals down, and post them where you can see them often.

2. **Create a document and copy the Recommendations you've written and ones you've received into this document.** Then use this document to draft future Recommendations without reinventing the wheel. I'm *not* saying to copy one Recommendation for someone else. There may be phrases that you could use for someone who is a leader or Expert in their field, and revise it or personalize it for someone else who is in a similar position.

3. **Keep on building your network. Make it a habit to think of how you can assist someone, thank them, and keep in touch.** It's especially important in building your network to contact people when you're not selling something or looking for something. A Giving and Collaborating mindset and attitude builds solid networks and relationships.

Action Steps for Tomorrow:

Make a list of professional and alumni organizations that you belong to or know about. LinkedIn has a Groups section where you can join these Groups. Tomorrow you'll look them up, and find new ones, too.

- _____

- _____

- _____

- _____

- _____

Day 7 – Special Areas of LinkedIn

15-20 minutes

DAY 7 – LinkedIn Groups – 15-20 minutes

LinkedIn Groups gives you an easy way to connect with people in groups of people who have something in common. You'll find communities of professionals who have a common experience, interest, affiliation or goal.

For example, you can connect with people in Groups including:
- Alumni groups
- Corporate groups
- Conference groups
- Networking groups
- Non-Profit groups
- Professional groups

You may be a member of a professional or networking organization where you live, and go to meetings there. Many of these organizations are national organizations that have local chapters. Now on LinkedIn, there are also online groups too.

One of the benefits of joining LinkedIn Groups is that you have a way to focus on areas where you have something in common with other LinkedIn members. It can be overwhelming to be a part of a community of 31+ million people. So in building your network, rather than trying to figure out who among LinkedIn's 31+ million members to connect with, you can start connecting with people who already have professional or other interests in common. It's also a way to keep up-to-date with what's going on in your industry or area of interest.

For me, I'm all about sales, CRM (Customer Relationship Management), networking and building relationships. I want to know people who are also in sales and sales technology, and who are committed to networking and building relationships. And I want to have good visibility and credibility in those areas. So a number of the LinkedIn Groups that I belong to are in those areas.

Think about your own goals and what you want LinkedIn to do for you. Review your answers from the Night Before chapter of this book. Ask yourself which types of Groups will be helpful to you in reaching your goals. Then go to the LinkedIn Groups Directory and search for groups.

Step 1 – Look up LinkedIn Groups in the Group Directory

Login to LinkedIn and start at the LinkedIn Home page.

1. **Go to Groups** (Click on *Groups* at the top left corner of the screen)

2. If you already are a member of groups, you'll see the logos and activities for the groups you belong to.

3. At the right side of the screen, you'll see Groups Directory. Click on *Find a Group*.

4. **Search for Groups of interest to you.** The easiest way to do that is to think of a professional, alumni or networking group you already belong to or know about. Type in the name in the Search Box. For example, type in the name of an organization in the search box. For now, leave the categories and languages as they are (All). A list of your search results will come up, and you can see if the organization you're looking for is there.

5. **Click on the Name** of a group, and you'll see the home page of the group with a description of the group, About this Group (on the right), and a listing of Group Members in your Network.

Step 2 – Join a Group

Join a group that makes sense. Click *Join Group*.

Some groups have an approval process, and when you join, a message goes to the Group Manager. You'll usually an approval in a few days or less. During that time your membership is "pending". When you join or are accepted, you'll see the group logo in your list of groups. When you're on the home page of the group, you can see discussions, news, updates, members and settings.

When your membership is pending, you'll see "pending" in your list of groups. You can send a message to the group manager right from this listing, or withdraw your request for membership.

When you are a member of a group, you can **take part in Discussions**, and see recent Discussions and Comments. You'll see a list of some of the discussions, and can see and participate in them.

From the list of Groups, **click on the name** of the group you want to look at. Then click on *Discussions*.

Click on the **title of the Discussion** you're interested in or want to comment on. Look at several discussions to get an idea of how they work, and think about how you want to participate.

Step 3 – Search for More LinkedIn Groups & Join

1. **Continue to search** for groups by name, and then search by category and key words. For example,

   Rather than searching a specific group by name, click on the arrow to the right of All Categories to see the types of groups in LinkedIn. You'll see a list that includes:
   - Alumni groups
   - Corporate groups
   - Conference groups
   - Networking groups
   - Non-Profit groups
   - Professional groups

1. **Select a category** such as Networking group. In the Search Box type in a key word for the area you're interested in. For example, type in sales, or marketing, or human resources, or financial services. Then click *Search*. You'll see a list of LinkedIn Groups that match that area. When I typed "sales" in the search box, a list of 2,739 groups came up.

2. **Browse** the list of Groups to see what's there, and which ones you want to join.

3. **Take time** over the next few weeks to look more carefully at these groups, and find people you want to connect with. When you find someone you want to connect with, invite them to be a part of your network. Remember to personalize your invitation message.

Insider Secrets:

1. **Join several LinkedIn Groups** where your target clients and decision-makers are, and then start connecting with people in those groups. Look at their Profiles and invite them if it seems to be a good connection for you. If you're not sure, pick up the phone and call them. People who know you're in the same group you're in are more likely to connect with you because you have that in common with them. Be active in the group discussions.

2. **Participating in Groups builds your credibility and visibility.**

3. Simply looking through the Groups Directory shows you **groups you probably didn't know existed.** You can also start a Group yourself.

Success Story:

The Success Story for how LinkedIn Groups work comes from my own experience. I've joined a number of sales and sales technology (CRM – Customer Relationship Management) groups. I recently got an e-mail from someone who said that we are in the same LinkedIn group. He said he was looking for potential business partners, saw my Profile, and wanted to talk. We did speak, and we will either work together or continue to network to help each other reach our goals.

The **real difference** that LinkedIn makes is that:

1. He found me easily because of the key words in my Profile and the LinkedIn Groups I belong to.

2. He looked at my Profile to see if I was an appropriate contact to assist him. He's looking for people with certain skills and experience, and mine matched. He saw that in my LinkedIn Profile, and contacted me. Because I'm in LinkedIn and have a Profile with the keywords for the types of skill and experience areas he's looking for in a business

partner, he found me. He most likely found a number of people the same way. We are in effect "pre-qualified" to be people for him to talk to.

3. We spoke, and are now networking.

4. Without LinkedIn, he would most likely not have found me and others who were already pre-qualified to talk with.

5. He might have started with a "cold" list of people, not knowing if they had the qualifications or interest. He might have spent a great deal of time researching and making calls to qualify them. For example, he could have purchased a mailing list. Then he would have spent a tremendous amount of time making calls and sending e-mails to people who couldn't help him or satisfy his criteria for a business partner. Or to find out that the person on the list was no longer in that position. Sound familiar?

6. With LinkedIn, the people who are there have already said that they want to be found and are committed to networking. You have a community of people at your finger tips.

As the commercial about Mastercard says,

- Finding people who can help you – that's good
- Contacting them – that's good

- Streamlining and getting fast results with LinkedIn – "*Priceless*"

Action Steps for Tomorrow:

1. **Power Up LinkedIn and Turn Up the Speed! And keep it going. Do at least 3 real-life searches and find 3 Groups to join.**

2. **Start networking today, and build your network on LinkedIn with 15-20 minutes a day.** Stay focused about what you want LinkedIn to do for you. Review your goals and Big Picture Worksheet you filled out at the beginning of this book.

3. You're now a LinkedIn Networker. Congratulations to you!

You now know the basics, and have the foundation of networking online with LinkedIn, and the skills to keep going. Keep your skills up and use LinkedIn almost every day. If you wonder how you can possibly add networking and LinkedIn to your already-busy day, read my article on *Finding Time*. You can get a copy for yourself by simply clicking on the link below or typing it into your browser: www.linkedinworks.com/resources/findingtime.pdf

.

Appendix A - Articles

Tips and Insider Secrets to get the Results you Want

in record time:

✓ **Find a job**

✓ **Find clients**

✓ **Be the recognized Expert**

Appendix A - Articles

10 Ways You Never Thought of Using LinkedIn
By Jan Wallen

When I've interviewed people for my program "Advice from the Experts", I found that people are using LinkedIn in unique ways. That inspired me to look everywhere to find unique and unusual ways that people are using LinkedIn. Here are 10 of the ways I've found so far. **If you're using LinkedIn in unusual and unique ways, tell me.** Call me at (877) 327-5058 or send an e-mail to me at: info@linkedinworks.com and put "New Ways" in the Subject line.

1. **Reverse check your manager and people you'll work with** before you accept a new position. When you're interviewing for a position, look up the person you'll interview with in LinkedIn. Get an idea of who they are, their interests, and their interests and career path. That way you'll be more prepared for your interview, and can start with a conversation and icebreakers rather than going in cold and not quite knowing what to say. As you progress in your interviews, look up the Profiles of the manager and people you'll be working with. You'll get an idea of what it will be like working there and with them. It also makes it easier during the interview because you're prepared. Look at their Recommendations. You could even contact other people who have worked with them.

2. **Update your network on your new business model, and as a result, getting calls and clients**. A colleague of mine who has a consulting business decided to change his business model. He wanted to work with clients on longer-term projects and have a greater impact on their top line and sales. He updated his LinkedIn Profile, and wrote a message to the people in his network that gave them an update on what he was doing now. He described the change he'd made in his business model, and mentioned the types of clients and projects he was looking for. He sent this update out to his network, and within a week, he received 5 calls from potential clients.

3. **Using LinkedIn with Google Alerts.** Look up people and companies you want to work with, potential clients and decision-makers or those where you want to work. Then to go Google and set up a Google Alert for those people and companies. You'll get a Google Alert in your Inbox telling you when those people and companies are in the press, or are doing something new. To set up Google Alerts, go to: alerts.google.com and follow the prompts. For example, if you want to know when a specific company is in the news, enter that company's name. Choose how often you want the alert, and you'll start receiving the alerts in your Inbox.

4. **Establishing your status as an Expert.** LinkedIn gives us the platform to spotlight our expertise, and be recognized as an Expert in the Answers area. Taking that a step further, you can write articles and have them picked up by many ezines and publications, which gives you visibility and credibility in addition to LinkedIn, blogs, Web sites and other social and marketing media. I've done this several ways, and now am very pleased with the results and services of SubmitYOURArticle. You can find out more about this on my Web site at: www.LinkedInWorks.com/resources.htm. The recommended length of articles is between 450-700 words, so it's easier now to write articles that reinforce your expertise. Remember to keep the readability at about a 5th or 6th grade level because comprehension and retention are significantly better at that level. An interesting study was done where doctors were asked to read medical articles that were written at college level, high school level and 7th grade level. They were tested for comprehension and retention of the material after reading each article. The doctors were skeptical, and thought it was "below them" to read high school and 7th grade level articles when they'd been reading at higher levels for so long. They were sure their scores would be better for the college level part of the test. The results showed that both comprehension and retention improved as the readability level decreased. And they were both significantly better when they read the material at the 7th grade level. It's easy to check the readability index of your articles in Microsoft Word. Send e-mail to me at: info@linkedinworks.com, and I'll send you the steps.

5. If you're **changing your career or industry, find a mentor**, do research and find someone in that industry who can answer your questions. Set up informational interviews to find out what it's really like to work in that new area, and decide if you really want to make the change. Clarify your expectations of what's involved.

6.   **Talk to people before you relocate.** For example, if your company is relocating, you can find real estate agents, services and service providers before you move. That way you can do things ahead of time rather than waiting until the last minute or until you're there. It makes things so smooth.

7.   **Get a job in a non-traditional way.** Update your resume and LinkedIn Profile. Then send a message out to your network saying, "I'm up for grabs!" (You might express it differently if that's not your style.) The fellow that did this said he had a new job in less than a week.

8.   **LinkedIn is international, too.** Find connections who can help you and where you can help them with their international goals. I've already made connections where they found me on LinkedIn from Hungary, India and South Africa, and we're continuing to network. I'll be actively pursuing this, and will give you an update on results and advice if you send an e-mail to me at: info@linkedinworks.com and put International in the Subject line.

9.   **Find people who have done similar projects**. Talk to them to see what it's like, gather information, and ask them for their advice. Save a tremendous amount of time by talking to someone who's already done what you want to do rather than learning it all on your own.

10.   **Get references for someone you're about to hire** – search companies where they worked in the past, and call them and ask for references.

And here's an ***extra tip for you*** – because I believe in *Lagniappe*, a New Orleans custom that means "a little bit extra". It started in New Orleans when the baker in New Orleans gave you an extra bun when you ordered a dozen. And I've adopted it and made it a part of my business practice.

11.   Find Experts and speakers for your programs and events. When you host meetings or events, go to LinkedIn to find Experts and speakers in your local area. You have a ready community of experts to choose from – all at your fingertips.

Networking Principles & Advice from the Experts
By Jan Wallen

To make it easier to really network with LinkedIn, and not simply collect connections like business cards that then sit in a stack on your desk, here are Networking Principles you can use when you meet people on LinkedIn or in person. These are my Top 3 Principles, ones that I've always made a part of my life. And there are more tips for you from networking Experts in the next few pages.

Adopt some of them yourself, and make them a part of your life so much that they come naturally to you and you don't even have to think about them. There are so many networking principles that it can be overwhelming. Pick one or two and start using them now.

Now with LinkedIn, these principles are even easier to follow than they ever were before. In a word, LinkedIn Works!

Networking Principle #1 -- "You must do it for yourself. You can't do it all alone."

I knew from a young age that working with people and getting results were always going to be important all my life. To do that successfully, I worked backwards from that principle and asked myself "What Will It Take" to do that?

One of the things was to know a lot of people I can serve and get results for, who can help me in my pursuits, are interesting and fun, people I can learn from, and who want to make a difference in the world, so I can make a contribution to them, too. I called this my Success Team. So I decided that one way to meet and connect with my Success Team people was to be able to meet and talk to a lot of people with diverse interests, backgrounds and ambitions.

So I set a goal for myself in college to be able to speak to anyone, anywhere, at any time about something substantive. That meant being a good conversationalist, and learning to ask thoughtful questions that would give me insights into the other person so I could understand them and talk to them about what interested them. It also meant knowing about many subjects, since I never knew before I met someone what they'd be interested in or what I could learn from them. I pursued this goal for many years, and in fact, I still do.

I also set a goal to give everyone I talk to something of value that would enhance their life or their work. Doing this is now a habit and is so automatic that it comes naturally in any conversation I have.

Networking Principle #2 -- *Jan's 10-foot Rule*. This has been one of *the* most valuable things I've ever adopted, and it works every time. *Jan's 10-foot Rule* is that you tell everyone within 10 feet of you what you're looking for, and someone comes through.

One of the best examples of this took place four years ago in Boulder, Colorado. My mother lives there in a retirement community. The staff called me on Memorial Day and said, "Can you come out here? Your mother is really not doing well." Of course! I was on a plane the next day. When I got to Boulder, I realized that it would be best for me to be there for the summer rather than commuting back and forth to New York. While I'd lived in Boulder and graduated from Boulder High, I hadn't kept in touch with people there. So to put *Jan's 10-foot Rule* in place, I talked to everyone within 10 feet of me -- the nurses, doctors and staff at the retirement community, my mother's friends, called my mother's church, and anyone else I could think of. I told them that I was looking for a place to house-sit for the summer.

Two days later, I got a phone call from someone I didn't know. She said that she'd heard from So-and-So, who knows So-and-So, that I was looking for a place to house-sit. I said that I was, and she asked if I wanted to come over and see the house. Her parents were away for the summer and they were looking for someone to house-sit. WOW!
And it gets even better. I told her I would like to see the house, and took down the address. It turns out that it was only two blocks from where my mother lives. I couldn't believe it! It could have been anywhere in Boulder! It was meant to be.

Everything worked well, and my mother's health definitely improved. I also spent the next summer there at their house. Then they returned, and I needed another place to stay for a couple of weeks. I put the word out again to everyone within 10 feet of me. Someone else I didn't know called and said that she had an extra guest room, and I was welcome to stay there.

With LinkedIn: You have a network and living community of people to ask – and they're all at your fingertips. They're not even 10' away.
Networking Principle #3 -- *Go where the fish are.* Over the many years that I've been networking, from college days onward, I've attended many networking and leads group meetings. I've been there as a guest, as a prospective member, and as

a speaker. What I found is that the members in a number of the groups that I visited were business owners who wanted to grow their business and were looking for clients. When they went to the meetings, they were meeting other business owners – business owners who were looking for clients. They weren't meeting their potential clients.

To be successful at networking, *go where the fish are*. That is, go to the meetings your potential clients attend. You won't get new clients if you're meeting other business owners. You may meet someone who can give you a referral, though for that to happen, they must be in touch with your potential clients and decision-makers.

With LinkedIn: **You have a network and living community of people who want to be found by other business people.** Find your decision-makers right here. Find the hiring managers. Find the Experts to speak at your events. You *are* where the fish are.

Networking Principles & Advice from More Experts

By Andrea R. Nierenberg

From *Savvy Networking: 118 Fast & Effective Tips for Business Success* – Andrea R. Nierenberg (Capital Books, Inc., 2007) For details, and to buy this book, go to www.linkedinworks.com/resources.htm. Andrea Nierenberg believes that networking is about giving first. This, her third book on the subject, is a gift to all who want to turn new contacts and prospective customers into warm relationships and lifelong customers – to grow, build, and keep your business.

Tip #4/ Open Your Eyes – Networking Is All Around

Research tells us there are at least two hundred people who are already part of your network. Get reacquainted with them. Networking is about creating and developing opportunities through meeting and "connecting the dots" among the people you know. The following ten categories of people can be the beginning of a great networking success story:

1. Customers or clients – they are the lifeblood of your business. Build trustworthy and positive relationships.
2. Suppliers – Refer to your supplier and improve your chances of staying on his/her radar screen.
3. Neighbors – Co-workers and colleagues – Office buddies are a powerful resource when networking. Invite a co-worker to lunch or coffee and get to know him/her better. Build your internal alliances.
4. People in your profession – Helping your competition can actually lead to greater opportunities to grow your business.
5. Former classmates – Seize the opportunities in your alumni magazine and pinpoint people who you might reconnect with.
6. Like-minded people – Expand your horizons. Extracurricular activities mean people with common inters and ambitions, or who shard similar life experiences.
7. Neighbors – Turn a friendly wave into an invaluable conversation. Get to know your neighbors. You can open up the door for new opportunity.
8. Friends – Take time to nurture and cultivate your friends. Network with them in a positive way, never with expectations.
9. Family – They can be a great resource for networking opportunities. Think of how you can be helpful those in your family.
10. People you meet by chance – Be kind to unfamiliar people. Airports, grocery store lines, and waiting rooms are filled with a world of networking opportunities. Keep your ears and eyes open. I learn something new every day by paying attention to the "universe".

Think of people you know who fit in each of these categories. The possibilities for networking are endless. Over time, as you build rapport and trust, these relationships lead to other contacts, partnerships, and opportunities.

Tip #96/ Polite Get-to-Know-You-Questions

These are examples of the kinds of open-ended, cordial questions that invite contacts to converse with you:

- If you could do any kind of work, what would it be, and what makes you say that?
- What do you do when you're not at work – family, hobbies or special interests?
- How did you get involved in this industry or group?

- What books or movies or plays have you seen recently?
- What do you like the most about your work and why?
- When you work with _____ (lawyers, bankers, consultants, etc.), what do you look for that makes your job and life easier?

Tip #97/ Nurturing, more Long-Range Questions

These are my all time favorites, which give me a reason to follow up and stay in touch – whether it will be on the short term or a long-range goal:

- How do I know when I'm either speaking to a potential client or job opportunity or person you would like to meet?
- What is your preferred method of communication for staying in touch?

It is only after I have asked, listened to, and understood their responses these questions that I can bring the conversation back to something about me. For example, when someone says, "We're looking for consultants who really customize their work to our company and stay on the project from beginning to end," I might say, "I totally agree with you, because when I recently worked with XYZ company, the leading reason I got the project was for customization, delivery, and follow through." Then I offer a short example of each.

The whole goal is getting people to open up so that they are talking about a subject near and dear to them, and we can develop cooperation and rapport. It is only by understanding people's needs that we can demonstrate sincere interest by basing our responses on them.

Jill Lublin and Rick Frishman

From *Networking Magic: Find the Best – from Doctors, Lawyers, and Accountants to Homes, Schools and Jobs* – Rick Frishman and Jill Lublin with Mark Steisel (Adams Media, 2004). Rick Frishman and Jill Lublin with Mark Steisel (Adams Media, 2004). For details, and to buy this book, go to www.linkedinworks.com/resources.htm. *Networking Magic* is a revolutionary concept that shows you how to find the best in all aspects of life. Whether you're looking for the most lucrative job, the highest-rated child care facility, the leading medical specialist, or virtually anything else – this is the one book that gets you on the inside track to the top experts, the highest-quality services, and the least expensive products.

Survey Says – Networking Do's

In the research for their book ***Networking Magic***, Rick Frishman and Jill Lublin surveyed a wide range of experienced networkers to find out what they considered their essential requirements for successfully networking with the best people. The answers that they saw most frequently are summarized below. The responses are arranged in a logical, orderly sequence that tracks the networking process.

1.   Believe that networking will work

Unless you are truly convinced your networking efforts will help you succeed, you will waste everyone's time. Positive energy translates into enthusiasm, which is contagious. The top people are usually excited about ideas. If they don't sense your excitement, they may not fully listen to you. Your belief in your cause will convince them to help you and to spread your message to others. . . .

2.   Target the right audience

Approach individuals who can provide what you seek or can direct you to those who can. Spend time carefully selecting and researching the best targets; the best people who can help you reach your goals. Then make a plan to meet them

If you plan to join groups and/or attend events, select those that target the people you want to reach. Get involved with several different network groups because a single group may not be able to satisfy all your needs, but don't spread yourself too thin. Sample different organizations and events in order to meet a different cross-section of people, but give them a chance. Circulating your name widely and putting it in play in a number of arenas can be extremely helpful.

3.   Make a strong first impression

Always put your best foot forward. You don't get a second chance to make a first impression, and a bad first impression can be ruinous.

Dress appropriately for those you hope to impress. Have a great sound bite, know your stuff, and be prepared to reel it off at any time and with confidence. Have a longer description of you or your business down pat that you can quickly recite in the event that you're asked about it.

4.   Network with those you emulate

Don't be afraid to approach people whom you admire and who inspire you. Shoot for the top. Meeting those who have achieved your goals gives you a blueprint to learn from and follow. Aim high and seek out those who will help you develop and grow.

While shooting for the top, don't abandon your peers. They can act as sounding boards and champion your causes.

5.   *Talk to everyone you meet*

Don't discount or overlook anyone. Be genuinely friendly. People remember your kindnesses to them and will go out of their way to reciprocate. When you give of yourself, even if it's only by talking to someone briefly, you're enhancing the possibility of building a relationship and getting something back. Develop a wide circle of friends and acquaintances from diverse fields.

6.   *Learn to read people*

Pay close attention and become skilled at sensing other people's needs. Learn to recognize who will give and who will only take. Trust your instincts and when they prove correct, increase your reliance on them. Learn to avoid those who only want to take because they will drain your time and energy.

7.   *Listen*

Listening can be an acquired skill, so work on becoming a good listener. Come away knowing one thing they like and one thing they dislike. Ask about their accomplishments before you tell them about yours. Be interested and curious. Don't take yourself too seriously, but take others very seriously.

8.   *Be waiting to help*

Give, give, give. Networking is a two-way street. Offer your help freely and generously. When others realize that you are willing to help and how generous you are, they will be eager to help you. Always keep your contacts' needs in mind and be alert for leads for your network partners. Go the extra mile to provide something special before asking for anything in return. Remember, networking is not only about you. ... "The reason most people are not successful networkers is that they prospect, instead of networking. Networking is being a valuable business and personal resource for others and EXPECTING NOTHING IN RETURN. The people who give the most will always receive the most." (Dave Sherman)

9.   *Be prepared*

Become an expert, and be able to provide insightful answers to questions about your field. If you truly want to network with the best, prove to them that you too want to become the best. Prepare by reading everything. Decide beforehand whom you want to meet and learn everything possible about them. Carry and hand out plenty of cares and literature about you and your business. Continue to learn, grow, and strive for success. Focus on building relationships and being rich in the resources of people. Also strive to fill the needs of others because, in time, you will reap the benefits.

10. Find common denominators

Common denominators are the thread that connects network partners. Without common interests, objectives, and values, bonds cannot be built. Connect in your mind anything that your contacts may have in common and then build upon those similarities. Common interests, backgrounds, and experiences make ideal ice-breakers and pave the way to building deeper, more lasting relationships.

11.   Bring value

Always have ideas, suggestions, and insights to share. Help the other person out first; don't wait for them to give you a lead or connection. Gain a reputation for generously giving value and you will never be alone or unappreciated.

12.   Be honest, courteous, and fair

Deliver what you promise and when you can, deliver more. Don't exaggerate or claim to be what you're not. Deliver on time, call on time, and show up on time. Become known for your reliability and dependability. Show others that they can always count on you. Always be fair and ethical; it will gain you respect, admiration, and tons of repeat business. Treat everyone with courtesy and respect and you will be treated with courtesy and respect in return. Build a great reputation. A terrific reputation is a commodity that endures, but that can be lost by just one lapse.

13.   Follow up

After you first meet someone, keep in touch in a creative way. Send special notes or postcards, ones that have significance to topics you discussed. Write information about your contacts' interests on the backs of their business cards. Then send them articles or information related to their interests.   Be quick to express your gratitude. Thank people with handwritten thank-you notes, e-mails, phone calls, or gifts. Distinguish yourself by promptly expressing your thanks.

14.   Keep referrers informed

As you build relationships, keep your network referrers in the loop. Let them know when you set up a meeting and fill them in on your progress. If you land a project, call them at once. And at each new step, express your thanks. Remember that those who have helped you have a stake in the outcome of introductions or connections they made on your behalf. By keeping them informed, you will be keeping them on your team and keeping them involved, where you can draw on their help and support.

15.   *Look at the big picture*

Try to see past the momentary, day-by-day activities that occupy your life and build toward your overall lifetime objectives. Sometimes taking nothing today will position you to gain far more tomorrow. Enlarge your perspective to see beyond immediate and constantly re-examine your long-term goals.

David Teten and Scott Allen

From The Virtual Handshake: Opening Doors and Closing Deals Online.
David Teten and Scott Allen (AMACOM 2005) For details, and to buy this book, go to www.linkedinworks.com/resources.htm. In *The Virtual Handshake*, David Teten and Scott Allen explain their Seven Keys to Powerful Network with clear real-life examples with you and several of your acquaintances.   Review these, and think about ways you can measure and build your own network. The first five of their seven keys measure the relationship between you and your acquaintances. And two measure the size and diversity of your network.

NOTE: The examples for each of the seven keys are from Table 2-1 in *The Virtual Handshake*.

The Seven Keys to a Powerful Network

To explain the Seven Keys to a powerful network, we will analyze a simple example. Let's assume that you are a lawyer living in Los Angeles, and you have a very simple network of three people: Armand, Brenda, and Chaim. *You know that your billing is driven by who you know. What exactly is the value of your network?*

1. **Character: Your integrity, clarity of motives, consistency of behavior, openness, discretion, and trustworthiness.** This is driven by the reality and the appearance: the real content of your Character, and what each Acquaintance thinks of your Character.

> Example: Armand and Chaim all think of you as a trustworthy, high-Character person. However, you have been late for several lunch appointments with Brenda and tend to gossip about various common friends with her. As a result, she thinks of you as unreliable and of mediocre Character.

2. **Competence: Your ability to walk your talk; your demonstrated capability.** It includes functional knowledge and skills, interpersonal skills, and judgment. Similarly, this is driven by both the real level of your Competence and by what each Acquaintance views as the level of your Competence.

> Example: Armand, Brenda and Chaim all know that you are an excellent lawyer. You have high perceived Competence.

3. **Relevance: The Acquaintance's value to You,** defined as the Acquaintance's ability to contribute to your own goals. The Acquaintance's Relevance is driven by the value of the Acquaintance's own network.

> Example: Armand and Brenda work for ExxonMobil Corporation, a potential client for your legal services. They are high Relevance. Chaim is an unpublished fiction writer, so he is low Relevance as a potential client.

4. **Information: The data you have about the Acquaintance.** First are the basic coordinates: e-mail address, phone numbers, family Information, and so on. Also invaluable is Information about his professional background, how his career is advancing, what coworkers say about him, what his likes and dislikes are, and so on.

> Example: You have current work and home telephone and e-mail information for Armand, Brenda and Chaim. In addition, because you see Armand and Chaim so often, you have current Information about their moods, how happy they are in their jobs, and all sorts of other useful background information.

5. **Strength: The closeness of the relationship between You and your Acquaintances.** This reflects the degree of trust and reciprocity between you.

> Example: You went to school with Armand and Chaim and have been close friends with them ever since. You go out once a month for dinner, so you have a high Strength relationship with them. You only see Brenda about twice a year; that relationship is low Strength.

6. **Number: How many people you know directly**, including both strong and weak ties.

> Example: You only have three people in your network, a very low Number.

7. **Diversity: Heterogeneity of your network** by geography, profession, industry, and hierarchical position. In addition, your network should ideally be Diverse by age, sex, ethnicity, political orientation, and so on.

> Example: Armand, Brenda, and Chaim are all of a different religious and cultural background than you. However, the three also all live in Los Angeles, and Armand and Brenda both work for the same company. On the whole, you have a modest level of Diversity.

Lovingkindness and Staying Connected

"Networking" has a bad name among some, in large part because it's perceived as being centered on how you can exploit others. On the contrary: true "networking" is finding how you can best help others. …

People resent being contacted only when you want to "use" them. They prefer at least the semblance (better yet the reality) of a long-term relationship. "[I]t takes about six or seven contacts with someone before they know who you are and before they have you in a marketplace niche in their mind," says career expert Lynne Waymon[1]. If you contact a person only when you have request, he or she is likely to have forgotten you, as well as resent the fact that you have connected first with a "take" instead of a "give".

So your objective is to help people, support them, and also ping them periodically so that they have you in mind. Here are some ideas on how to do this:

Provide business leads. E-mail your friend to point out people in online communities whom they should meet

Recognize and share successes. Mail your group with the good news!

Mentor a young person. Make sure to register as an alumni advisor with your university.

Send an invitation to join a virtual community or participate in an online conference or blog.

Send a thank you note for something the person sent you.

Contact the person to ask for advice on something (for example, a company you are finalizing, equipment purchase you are researching). This makes the person feel respected and authoritative, and it has built-in follow-up: you contact the person later to let the person know how the recommendation worked. Of course, the request should be sincere and appropriate.

Send an e-mail with a link to an interesting article or Web site. It's valuable to maintain a file of areas of common interest of your friends. For example, keep a short list of the e-mail addresses of all the people that you know who work in the pharmaceutical industry. Whenever you come across news or information relevant to the pharmaceutical industry, you can easily forward to those people with a simple cut and paste. You might also keep lists by interest: Friends looking to get married, Democratic friends, Pakistani friends, etc.

Observe what's important to them. Send a St. Patrick's Day card to an Irish client or a Happy Chinese New Year card to a Chinese friend. These are far more noticeable and appreciated than a generic "Happy New Year" card.

Speak their language. If you have a Turkish friend, search online for "Turkish Happy Birthday and you can then learn how to wish your friend "Dogum gunun kutlu olsun!"

Observe organizational/personal/company changes and send notes of congratulations. Send a note regarding an award the person received. Write to say you enjoyed reading about his/her company profiled in a magazine.

Send an announcement when your company or you are recognized in some way. However, this tactic should not be over-used, to avoid excessive self-promotion.

Report any major change in your situation: marriage, promotion, or a new phone number.

Send e-cards. Blue Mountain (BlueMountain.com) and Yahoo! Greetings (Greetings.Yahoo.com) both provide free and low-cost options for sending cards; JacquieLawson.com offers a more expensive, higher-impact card. We always recommend customizing a card, paper or electronic, by writing a unique note on it. As a general rule, the more time and effort (not necessarily money) that you invest in a gift, the more it's appreciated. Since paper cards are labor-intensive to prepare and send, they have a greater impact than e-cards.

[1] Lynne Waymon, quoted in ExecuNet, *ExecuNet's Career Guide. Networking Knowledge: Techniques and Strategies to Help You Build Your Lifetime Network* (Norwalk, CT: ExecuNet Inc., 2002). To our knowledge, there is no particular academic research supporting or refuting this claim.

[2] Includes some ideas from Harvey Mackay, *Dig Your Well Before You're Thirsty* (New York: Doubleday, 1999)

More Articles by Jan Wallen:

FAQs – Frequently Asked Questions

1. **WII-FM? What's In It For Me? -- The Universal Radio Station**

   - ✓ What will LinkedIn do for me as a person?
   - ✓ Why should I use it?
   - ✓ What will it do for my career and business?
   - ✓ What is social networking and what can it do for me?

   In thinking about how to answer the questions that many people ask me, I thought about my life B.L. (Before LinkedIn). I've been networking and building relationships all my life. I'm a firm believer in it, and have seen successes that would never have happened otherwise. So to start answering these questions, here's what LinkedIn can do for you.

Before I answer the questions, I'll tell you that I'm biased. I'm now such a LinkedIn Evangelist that I can't imagine being without it – *ever*. Why? Because LinkedIn Works!

Here's the Executive Summary of how I use LinkedIn. You can also see more of what LinkedIn can do for you in the chapter "10 Ways You Never Thought of Using LinkedIn".

✓ **Connect with business people** when I'm in a beautiful rural area with fewer business people and great distances between in-person meetings.

✓ **Lead generation and prospecting for clients.** I do this in a much more targeted and streamlined way with LinkedIn. I find decision-makers who are in my target market audience, and before I contact them, I read their LinkedIn Profile and get to know something about them. I read the Company information in LinkedIn, and know a lot more about their company. And I combine that knowledge with Google Alerts about them and their companies, and challenges in the marketplace. That way I'm not spending time cleaning up a database, mailing list or cold calling.

✓ With LinkedIn I am proactive, seeking out potential clients that fit my target audience and the profile of my Ideal client. Some potential clients find me in LinkedIn, also. It focuses your prospecting and lead generation, whereas the Internet or world in general is a huge unmanageable size.

✓ **Product and service development.** I contact decision-makers and colleagues and talk to them about new products and services to develop. This market research helps me develop products and services that my target audience wants and will pay for, thus saving a tremendous amount of time and effort.

✓ **Preparation for sales calls and visits – never cold call again.** (See Lead generation above)

✓ **Mutual referrals.** Someone on LinkedIn found me and wanted to connect because we provide different types of services in the same industry, and can most likely refer people to each other. I've made a habit of referring people to others in my network.

✓ **Professional development.** I learn about people, events, and programs where I can stay up-to-speed in my industry and on topics of interest to my target audience.

✓ **Strategic alliances, business partnerships, joint ventures and consulting opportunities.** Several people on LinkedIn have found me in LinkedIn Groups. Now we're either working together, continuing to network or planning projects.

✓ **Helping people in my network find jobs and new positions.** I've referred and connected people in my network to others who can assist them, and I've shown them ways to use LinkedIn in creative and unique ways to pursue their job search.

2. **What do People Say About Using LinkedIn?**

LinkedIn is quickly becoming an indispensable tool for business people if your business depends on making the right connections. I've interviewed many business people and professionals about how they use LinkedIn, and what they find most valuable in using it. Here's what they say about how they use LinkedIn:

- Recruiters are using it to **find candidates**
- Marketing executives are using it for **business development** –
- Job hunters are using it to **find jobs** and connect with people in companies before openings are announced
- Salespeople are using it to **build relationships** and business, to **prepare for sales calls** and **streamline their sales process**
- More and more **jobs are requiring the skill** of social networking
- Business Owners are using it to **build their brand**
- Corporate executives are using it to **build their visibility and credibility** in their areas of expertise
- Many people are using it to **keep in touch** with colleagues from companies where they worked, and to keep up with school colleagues
- LinkedIn members are using it to **stay in touch** and **up-to-speed** in their industries, **exchange knowledge** and advice, **build a network before they really must have one** (for example, before layoffs or a slow economy), and to recession-proof their business

3.   What is Social Networking? Why should I know about it?

According to Wikipedia (www.Wikipedia.com)

"Social networking has created new ways to communicate and share information. Social networking websites are being used regularly by millions of people, and it now seems that social networking will be an enduring part of everyday life. The main types of social networking services are those which contain directories of some categories (such as former classmates), means to connect with friends (usually with self-description pages), and recommender systems linked to trust.

A **social network service** focuses on building online communities of people who share interests and activities, or who are interested in exploring the interests and activities of others. Most social network services are web based and provide a variety of ways for users to interact, such as e-mail and instant messaging services." *Wikipedia, 2008*

Social networking is very similar to the in-person and telephone networking that we're used to. For example, we have hiking groups, book clubs, social clubs, church groups, town communities and alumni groups wherever we live, and we can participate in them. Networking is not simply collecting business cards or a number of connections. When you really network, you get to know people, build relationships and help each other out. Online social networking is similar.

How do you know which online network to participate in? That depends on what you want to do there, who you want to meet and connect with, and what you want the group to do for you. Some popular sites are primarily for socializing rather than for business. LinkedIn is the premier online network for business. It's perfect for business people who want to connect with other like-minded business people who have interests in common.

Companies are now hiring people to keep an eye on the social networking sites to see what people are saying about their company so they can handle anything that comes up that may affect the company negatively, and so there will be no surprises. Companies are also looking for job search candidates who use social networking. It is definitely in your interest to learn to use LinkedIn and know about other social networking sites.

10 ½ Ways to Optimize your LinkedIn Profile
By Jan Wallen

Your LinkedIn Profile is like your resume and more! – People will find you when they're looking for products and services, for top talent to fill positions, for jobs, and for answers. You'll also look for these same things when you search LinkedIn. Your Profile is your "first impression". You don't have a second chance to make a first impression, so make your LinkedIn Profile compelling. Here are some tips to optimize your Profile:

1. **Before** you go to LinkedIn to create your Profile, think about your **Big Picture Vision of your career and life.** Write down the answers to these key questions:
    - ✓ What is your expertise and what are you known for?
    - ✓ What do you want people to ask you for now? What do you want to be known as the Expert in?
    - ✓ When people think of Tiger Woods, they immediately think of "golf". What do you want them to think of when they think of you?

    My Big Picture Worksheet gives you a snapshot of your Ideal vision for your career or business. To get your copy, click on the link below or type it into your browser: www.linkedinworks.com/resources/bigpicture.pdf

2. Have your resume handy as you write your LinkedIn Profile. You want to be complete, especially about your responsibilities and results you've achieved. **Be sure your resume is results-oriented, and update it to include your current position and work.**

    A big mistake people make with their LinkedIn Profile is making it exactly like their resume – backwards-oriented. That is, only showing what you've done in the past. With your LinkedIn Profile, **be sure it also reflects what you're doing now and what you want to do.** For example, if you're a start-up business looking for funding or investors, be sure everything that a potential investor looks for in a company is in your Profile. Or if you're looking for a job, be sure that everything a potential employer is looking for in a job candidate is in your Profile.

3. Think of **keywords** that people might search on to find you. For example, if you're looking for a job, some relevant key words might be:
   - Your current job title
   - The title of the position you're looking for
   - Your functional responsibilities. When I sold an accurate database of executives that companies used for their marketing, the database could be searched by "Job Function" as well as title. For example, the job title was Vice President, and Job Functions were Financial, Sales, Marketing, HR, etc.

   Or if you want to find more clients, some keywords you'd use to find the person you're looking for would be their current job title or industry, or the names of services they're looking for (training, consulting, branding, etc.).

4. Be sure the **photo** you put up on LinkedIn is a good one, and shows you as the executive and professional that you are. If you don't have a photo that's a good representation of you as you are now, it's worth to get a new one. Remember, your Profile is the first impression people will get of who you are.

5. **Add your personality** to your LinkedIn Profile. When someone sees your LinkedIn Profile, make it stand out so you stand out from the crowd. Make your Profile a representation of you – not simply an electronic resume.

6. When your LinkedIn Profile is complete, it's **searchable by the search engines** – almost like your own Web page. Look at other peoples' Profiles before you create yours. There are good examples to look at to get ideas for what to include in your Profile. Check out Profiles of several people in your industry or area of expertise, and some that are outside your area.

7. **Ask for Recommendations** as soon as your Profile is finished. Ask people who know you to write a Recommendation for you. Perhaps people from the company where you work, or clients, if you have your own business. Recommendations are like testimonials about you, and can include how you've worked together, results you've achieved, and why someone likes working with you. A good way to get Recommendations is to offer to write one for people you know on LinkedIn. Many times they'll offer to write one in return.

8. Make a **list of your goals and what you want to accomplish from being a part of LinkedIn**. There's an Interests section of your Profile where you list why you're a part of LinkedIn, and what you want to get from it. For example, business opportunities, a new job, let people know about your business or special events, etc.

9. Make it a habit to **use LinkedIn before you travel.** Search for people in the city you're traveling to, and connect with them via LinkedIn, a phone call or via e-mail. Send them the link to your Profile, and tell them you're in LinkedIn and want to meet with them when you're in their city. Solid networks are being built in person through LinkedIn.

10. **Include the link to your LinkedIn Profile in your e-mail signature**, so people can click right through to see your Profile. Also include in the resource box of articles you write. Be sure you personalize it before you start sending it out. For example, rather than the link that LinkedIn gives you automatically, which is something like, www.linkedin.com/in/146t25ab, personalize it so people can read it and know it's you. (It's easy). For example, mine is www.linkedin.com/in/janwallen. To receive my article "Step 2 – Your Vanity URL" that shows you how to personalize the link to your LinkedIn Profile, send an e-mail to me at info@linkedinworks.com and put Vanity URL in the Subject line.

And here's **_extra tip for you_** – because I believe in _Lagniappe_, a New Orleans custom that means "a little bit extra". It started in New Orleans when the baker gave you an extra bun when you ordered a dozen. And I've adopted it and made it a part of my business practice.

Your _Lagniappe:_

10.5 **Connect** with people you know and want to know on LinkedIn. Invite people to be a part of your LinkedIn network. It's very easy to extend an invitation – there's an e-mail that LinkedIn has already created to invite someone to be a part of your network. I highly recommend **personalizing your invitation** rather than use the rather bland one that was written by LinkedIn. For example, say something about why you want to connect, who you are and how you see networking with them.a

The Top 5 Secrets to Making LinkedIn Work
By Jan Wallen

1. **Be sure your Profile reflects your current purpose and what you want to accomplish by using LinkedIn**

    One mistake that many LinkedIn users make is to simply jump into doing searches and sending out invitations without taking time to think about what they want to accomplish in using LinkedIn. When you take time to do think it through, you'll be much more efficient and effective using LinkedIn. For example, if you're using it to find a job, be sure your Profile is complete, results-oriented, and shows the recruiter or hiring decision-maker why hiring you is in their best interest. And be sure that your LinkedIn Settings make it possible to view your entire Profile.

    Here are some things to think through and questions to answer before your start using LinkedIn and create your LinkedIn Profile:

    o **Be sure your LinkedIn Profile is results-oriented** like a resume, and also shows your personality, style and who you are. Your LinkedIn Profile is not a C.V. (curriculum vitae). It's more.

    o **Think about who will see your Profile**. Other LinkedIn members are doing searches and finding your Profile. What do you want them to see? They could be recruiters, business owners and decision-makers who want to buy your products and services, fellow LinkedIn members who are traveling and who want to meet in person when they're traveling to your city.

    o **Have your resume handy when you create your LinkedIn Profile.** It's the starting point for your LinkedIn Profile. Your Profile is more than a resume – it shows your style and personality more than a resume does. That's what you want because people connect with people. Review your resume and answer these questions:

*   Does your resume suit your current purpose? Your LinkedIn Profile is dynamic, and you'll change it over time to reflect your current purpose in using LinkedIn.

    _____   YES   _____ NO

- What do you want to add or remove to make it better fit your current purpose?

_____

_____

_____

_____

For example, if you're starting a **job search**, is your resume updated and does it reflect the type of position you're looking for?

- If you're in a **new position** and want to advance your career or use LinkedIn for your current company, does your resume reflect what you're currently doing?

- If you're a **business owner**, does it show how your background fits with your current business, products and services? And does it show what your business offers – i.e., the services and Value you offer?. Does it differentiate your business from others who do similar things?

- If you're **establishing your personal and professional brand**, does your resume outline your expertise? Does it show how you're the Expert in that area?

o **When you send Invitations write a personalized message.** For example, LinkedIn gives you an automatic impersonal message to use when you send an Invitation that says, "I'd like to invite you to connect . . ." Rather than using that impersonal message, write your own personal message. Say why you want to connect, and perhaps some things you have in common. When you update your Profile and let your connections know about the updates, LinkedIn also gives you a bland impersonal message. Personalize that one, also.

o **Decide what your social networking strategy will be.** Do you want many, many connections with people you don't know well? Or do you want to know all of your connections, and not accept every invitation you receive? You may see the terms Open networker and LION?

o **Decide which e-mail address you'll use for your LinkedIn connections.** If you change your e-mail address, go to your Account Settings and add the new address and make it your default e-mail address. Keep the old e-mail address listed in LinkedIn, because people still have it.

2. **Really network and know your connections – pick up the phone.** LinkedIn gives you the technology structure to really leverage your social network and connections. It's not meant to be a way to stay at a distance from your connections. Pick up the phone and talk to them. If you receive an invitation to connect from someone you don't know, pick up the phone. Talk to them. Tell them that you're not comfortable accepting their invitation because you don't know them yet. Talk about how you can help each other, and get to know them. Then accept their invitation if you're comfortable.

3. **Leverage your network and build social capital.** To really make LinkedIn work for you, go into it with the attitude of being there to help other members. Be proactive in networking. When you introduce yourself and follow up with people, be the first to offer to do something for them. If you're asking them for Recommendations or connections, tell them that you'll do something for them in the future (and do it!), and ask what you can do for them. A real turn-off is someone who networks with a "gimme, gimme, gimme" attitude. You're on LinkedIn to be a giver, not a taker.

4. **Know the Terms of Service and abide by them,** or your account can be suspended. As of this writing, they are available on the LinkedIn Web site: www.LinkedIn.com.

5. **Make a commitment to networking every day.** Networking and being on LinkedIn for as little as 15 minutes a day gets results. You may increase this at times where you're looking for a job, looking for new markets for your products and services, or working on a special project. The consistency of networking is what really makes the difference. I highly recommend doing your networking at the same time each day. That way it becomes a habit, and your brain gets used to the routine. So it's faster to network every morning or every evening than it is to do it sometimes in the morning and sometimes in the evening. I find that it works best for me to spend 15 minutes in the morning and 10-15 minutes at the end of the day. I spend a few minutes with my cup of coffee thinking about who I'll network with or the searches I'll do, and then at the end of the day I'll send out invitations to connect, or do what I said I'd do to follow up with people. That also ends the day with success and on a good note. I also make a habit at the end of each day to connect with appropriate people I spoke with during the day.

What if you're too busy? If you're so busy, you don't have time to network, take a look at your day, and see what you're really accomplishing. What I see with my clients is that some are working on a ToDo list rather than on projects. A project has a start, activities, tasks and milestones to accomplish, and a finish. Your projects roll up into the goals you're working toward. If your ToDo list is longer than your day, you never seem to get everything done, and you feel as though you're not getting anywhere, *STOP*. Take 10 minutes and clear your mind. Write down everything you can think of that's on your ToDo list, things you want to do, and things you'd love to do if you only had time. Now look at your list, and see what items are related and could be combined into a project, and which ones roll up to your yearly goals. Then decide when you'll finish your project. Put a "By When" date on it. If your projects don't roll up into your yearly goals, stop doing them or do them later in the year. Organize the activities in order and get going on your project. Projects get completed, and you get the satisfaction of completing something. ToDos seem to pile up and pile up. You get no satisfaction, and there's always so much more to do that it can weigh you down.

If you're still not accomplishing as much as you want to, take a look at my article "Finding Time" and the "Laser Focus" time organization system I've developed. To get your copy of the article I wrote go to www.LinkedInWorks.com/resources.pdf or send an e-mail to me at info@linkedinworks.com and put Finding Time in the Subject line. We'll send it right off to you.

The 5 Biggest Selling Mistakes & How to Avoid Them
By Jan Wallen

1. Not Mastering Following Up!

The most successful salespeople and entrepreneurs are the ones who have really mastered Follow-Up. Yes, the sales presentations and Elevator Speeches are important. Mastering Follow-Up is what makes the sales happen.

Here's what I mean:

People must have at least 7-16 contacts from you before they buy. This is especially true if you're selling services like consulting and high-ticket services and products. Be sure you're in front of them throughout the year, *especially* when they're ready to buy.

And here's what it means to your sales if you don't follow up:
(Look at the number here, and do the math! YIKES!)

70% of all buyers surveyed say that, when a purchasing need arises, it's unlikely that salesperson has recently called [them]. (Gartner, Yankee Group)

For Results: Master Follow-Up.

✓ **Send e-mails on a regular basis**, consistently throughout the year, so your message and results are on their radar screen. This can be automated with autoresponders where e-mails can be scheduled to go out on specific dates. The best way is to design a series of e-mails that give valuable information and tips throughout the year. You can use an autoresponder to set up the series of messages. The one I use is excellent, and very easy to set up and use. To find out more about it, go to www.LinkedInWorks.com/resources.html.

✓ **Send cards and postcards.** This is even better than e-mail now, because we all get so many e-mails. And people love to open cards. I've found a way to do this very easily for my own business, and do it without even having to go to the store to buy cards or post office to buy stamps. Now I do it all right at my desk, and it's so easy I send cards every day. Call me at (877) 327-5058, and you can send out a free card to try it out.

✓ **Call them back even if they don't return the calls.** Give them valuable information each time you call. Remember how busy people are – we all are. I've made it a habit for years to call them and check in. Buyers usually tell me how much they appreciate my patience and persistence. How many times is "too many"? Call them back until they tell you "Don't ever call me again!" (I've never had anyone tell me that! Ever.)

2. Talking about the price before you've shown them the Value

People decide who to hire and what to buy based on price (the lowest price) IF every company, product or service appear to be the same.

People will pay a premium price for something they see as valuable to them, and that will solve their Challenges.

If you talk about price before Value, they have no choice except to choose on the basis of price (the lowest price).

For Results: Talk about Value from the start. Tell them in your initial conversation and your Elevator Speech how your products and services get results and bring bottom-line value to them. Show them how your products and services are different from others who do similar things. show them with examples and client stories.

3. Looking the Same as Other Companies that Offer Similar Things

People Choose the Lowest Price if Everything Looks the Same (Haven't you done that, too?)

For Results:

- *Differentiate yourself from others who do similar things. Be Positively Memorable! Stand out Positively in their mind – create pictures of what it's like to work with you with examples and client stories.*
-
- *Show them the Value! Talk about the Value in your first conversation – not only when they're ready to buy.*

4. MEGO (My Eyes Glaze Over) Elevator Speeches & Presentations

What are MEGO Elevator Speeches and Presentations??
o   When you say your Elevator Speech, you tell people a menu of what you do, all the places you work and all the clients you've worked with – ever. You do that hoping they'll see something they like and call you to buy it. It won't happen! Their eyes glaze over in boredom.

You show them a Power Point presentation with slide after slide after slide after slide. The biggest mistake is to give a Power Point presentation after lunch with the lights down. (!)

They are "Me" oriented – for example,
*   "We're the best."
*   "We believe your company should do . . ."
*   "We work with top companies . . ."

For Results: Make it compelling – tell them who your clients are, the results you get for your clients, and create a picture in their mind. Here are two examples of what a Financial Planner could say:

1)
"Hello, I'm Joe Smith. I'm a Financial Planner. I put together financial plans for people."

(This one doesn't pass the "So What?!" Test.)

2)
"Hello, I'm Jane Sampson. I manage business owners' finances so they can retire 2-3 years earlier than they thought they could." (What?! You mean I can retire 2-3 years earlier than I thought I could?! Wow! When can we start?)

When you hear both of these Elevator Speeches, which financial planner do you want to work with?

5. Using the Hard-Sell or "Buy *NOW!* (or else)" Approach

Pressure and the hard-sell approach will work sometimes -- maybe. Not many. And it really puts people off. You see this approach a lot on the Internet, especially on the sales pages for information products. For example,
- o "Learn how to write "Killer Copy" for your Web site and sales pages
- o "Only 5 spots left!" (in the seminar or teleseminar)
- o "This is your last chance – buy now or you'll miss out"

For Results: Talk to people as people – intelligent, thoughtful people who have a challenge to solve, and want to make an intelligent, thoughtful decision. People who want the information and options so they can make a decision. Show them the Value of working with you – be sure they can answer "What's In It For Me?" Always give them a CTA (Call to Action), and agree on Next Action Steps.

Target Practice – Riches Are Niches
By Jan Wallen

This is the transcript from one of my radio shows on how to *Turn What You Know Into Cash Flow Now*™. It's about how to find your target audience and Niche market. And it's what I call Target Practice.

Hello and Welcome to the Turn What You Know into Cash Flow Now™ radio show.

I'm your host – Jan Wallen. It's great to be with you today.

We're talking more today about how you can make more money than you are now – even twice as much -- **without working twice as hard – all from what you already know.**

Today we'll continue with how to find your perfect Niche and be seen as the recognized Expert in your Niche. So you can *Turn What You Know into Cash Flow Now*™.

Your audience and your Niche are critical to your success and being known as a leading expert. Your goal is to sell highly profitable information products to people who really want to buy them.

Exactly what is a Niche?

A Niche is a specific group within your target audience and clients. For example, a business that provides marketing services may have a target audience of "business owners" because business owners always want to get more clients.

For example,

A Niche within "business owners" is "business owners who are speakers" or "business owners of companies that have been in business at least 3 years" or "owners of companies who want annual sales of 10 million-dollars".

Here are some examples of descriptions for your potential Niche:

Doctors – This is **too broad!**

Doctors who specialize in cardiology -- **Good**

Doctors who specialize in diabetes and whose practice is in major New York metro area hospitals – This is **best** because it's very specific

The way I describe a Niche is: An inch wide and a mile deep.

Once you define your perfect Niche, you'll be finding and solving their biggest challenges – the ones they'll do almost anything and pay almost anything to solve.

Then you'll be providing the solutions to those challenges. Here are 3 things you can do *now* to find and solve their challenges, and be seen as the recognized Expert in your field.

Step 1 - Find the words they use to express their pains, ambitions and solutions they are looking for

1. Listen to your audience. Use *their* language – Time management <u>vs</u>. "more time with family"

Coaches talk about "multiple streams of income", speakers talk about "getting more product"   Look at "www.stopyourdivorce.com" vs. "build relationships"

2. Read the magazines they read. Visit Web sites they'd visit. Check out the headlines of articles – these are their pains, ambitions, and solutions they're looking for. Ask them what they're concerned about and see which words they use. Remember, you're looking for the words that people in your Niche use to describe their challenges – NOT words that you, as the knowledgeable Expert would use.

3. Steer clear of industry jargon, technical terms and buzzwords that people outside your industry may not understand.

How can you find these words that people in your target audience use? Look at Web sites, professional organizations and publications that people in your Niche are likely to look at and read. Look at conferences they attend, and the books and magazines they read, and check out the headlines.

Another way is to Google words that people in your Niche might use when they look for answers to their challenges. For example, If people in your Niche want better relationships, to go Google and type in "relationship", "relationship help", "better relationship" or "relationship expert". If people in your Niche are stressed out, type in "stress", "stress management" or "stress management expert". You'll see lists of companies and people that solve these challenges. If there are a lot of these listed, you have a pretty good indication that people want to solve these challenges. Look at Web sites and publications that your Niche might read. Check out the headlines. These also tell you about their challenges. And if they're in industry and well-known publications, chances are good that a lot of people in their audience want to solve these challenges. Subscription consulting or CD – described this one quite in depth

Step 3 – Use their challenge in your Elevator Speech

A worksheet is available for this section. To get your copy, go to www.linkedinworks.com/resources/elevatorspeech.pdf.
- Use these 3 components in your Elevator Speech, and paint a picture in their mind of what you can do for them.
    o Who your clients are – your Niche
    o What you do for them – the results you get for them
    o The Value you provide – what it means to them

For example, **compare**: "Hello, I'm Joe Smith. I'm a Financial Planner."

To

"Hello, I'm Joe Smith. I show business owners how they can retire 2-3 years earlier than they thought they could."

Break down the elements – show each one in the above Elevator Speech and why to do each one, why each one is important. Use the Elevator Speech Worksheet to do this.

Step 3 Market to your target clients consistently

- Follow-up, Follow-up, Follow-up! – Use autoresponders like EasyWebAutomation (for more information, go to www.linkedinworks.com/resources)

- Automate your marketing – **Use autoresponders to send a series of messages to your clients and prospective clients on a regular basis. Design a series of e-mails and mailings that you send throughout the year.**

- It takes at least ___**7-16**___ contacts before people buy from you.

We'll devote an entire show to autoresponders, shopping carts and automating your marketing.

Before our time is up --

Your Call to Action:

Write down your Top 3 Next Steps to finding *your* Riches in Niches?

1. _____

2. _____

3. _____

Be sure to put the "BY WHEN" date for each of these – it's SO important in actually getting things done.

Appendix B - Resources for You

These are resources that I've discovered and are the most popular with my clients. I also use them myself. I'm telling you about them so that you can reach your goals and build the career and business that you want to in the easiest way possible.

Articles & Tools

Jan's Big Picture Worksheet -- This worksheet gives you a Helicopter View of your ideal career, business and life outside work. My clients find that it clarifies their goals and makes it easier to see their longer-term vision. They refer to it often throughout the year. It's brief, and gives you a snapshot of your current situation and goals. Think about both your personal and professional goals and how you want LinkedIn to help you achieve them. You can get a copy of the worksheet by clicking the link or typing it in your browser: www.linkedinworks.com/resources/bigpicture.pdf

The Most Important 10 Minutes You'll Spend in LinkedIn -- This is an article I wrote after I learned that someone's LinkedIn Profile was accidentally deleted from LinkedIn. Follow these steps ASAP. If you know people who don't know about backing up your LinkedIn network, tell them right away. They can get a copy of the article by simply clicking the link or typing it in their browser: www.linkedinworks.com/resources/10minutes.pdf

You've spent a lot of time and given a lot of attention to your LinkedIn Profile. And when you're using LinkedIn to network and build your business, enhance your career with a new position, or find your next superstar employee, you have valuable information and connections at your fingertips. Take time *now* to back it up. **Your network is priceless . . . Protect it.**

10.5 Ways to Optimize Your LinkedIn Profile – Your LinkedIn Profile is your presence in LinkedIn. You can't do anything in LinkedIn until you have your Profile up. And your Profile is how people decide whether to connect with you, consult with you and your company or hire you if you're doing a job search. Your LinkedIn Profile is also like your personal Web page because the search engines also search your LinkedIn Profile when it's completed, and you can use the link to your LinkedIn Profile in your e-mail signature. It's an important sales piece. **If you know people who are looking for jobs or who will be looking soon, tell them to call me so they can start using LinkedIn ASAP. They must get on LinkedIn ASAP and create their Profile in a way that highlights who they are, shows off their skills and the results they get, and differentiates them from others that recruiters or hiring managers may find in their search results.**   This article shows them how to do exactly that.   They can get a copy of the article by simply clicking the link or typing it in their browser: www.linkedinworks.com/resources/10waystooptimize.pdf

Finding Time when You're Already Too Busy -- You now know the basics, and have the foundation of networking online with LinkedIn, and the skills to keep going. If you wonder how you can possibly add networking and LinkedIn to your already-busy day, read my article on Finding Time. You'll have the answer. You can get a copy for yourself by simply clicking the link or typing it in your browser: www.linkedinworks.com/resources/findingtime.pdf

Services: For details, to check them out, and sign up for them, go to my Web site www.linkedinworks.com/resources.htm

SubmitYOURArticle

Submit Your Article to thousands of publishers and generate massive publicity for your Web site via this automated article submission service. It's easier than you think. You simply write your article (only 450-700 words), submit it, and it will be distributed to targeted publishers and article directories across the globe, within seconds. They submit your articles to major article directory hubs that attract several thousand publishers a day, to category-specific web sites, and to high-quality publishers on our in-house list who have requested to receive your article submissions. Doing this manually would take you hours ... we do it for you automatically, in seconds. Set up a Google Alert for your name, and you'll see where your articles have been published. For details, go to my Web site www.linkedinworks.com/resources.htm

Easy Web Automation Shopping Cart and Autoresponders

What I like best about EasyWebAutomation is: It puts everything in one place. Because my shopping cart and autoresponders are all together in EasyWebAutomation, 1) it's easy to track my orders and be sure that customers get their products and special announcements easily. 2) It's easy to find Virtual Assistants and Web designers who already know how to use it. (Even if they don't, it's very easy for them to learn it, and very easy to call Customer Support and have a real person help out.) 3) Even best for me – I only have one application and one person to manage. My colleagues who have their autoresponders and shopping carts as two different programs, have to manage both (and two people if their Virtual Assistants manage their autoresponders and shopping cart for them). This saves me tons of time! Best yet, you can try it out for yourself for only $3.95!

"EasyWebAutomation is the #1 Automation and Shopping cart solution for businesses that are serious about making money online." - *Jay Conrad Levinson, author of Guerrilla Marketing.* For details, go to my Web site www.linkedinworks.com/resources.htm

BYO Audio

With BYO Audio: 1) Adding audio to your Web site is a snap. Just select the audio you want posted to your website from the list of audios you've recorded, and customize the play button the way you want it. They *generate the HTML source code* for you that can be copied and pasted into your web page. So it's just choose, cut, paste . . . that's it. 2) You can make pre-designed audio postcards to e-mail to friends and business associates. 3) Record your audios from anywhere anytime. Their browser-based audio recorder runs on virtually any other desktop operating system. This means consistency and maximum flexibility when you need it. *You may also call their Media Center* and listen to, re-record, and create new audios using your telephone, 24 hours a day, 7 days a week. It really *does not get easier than this.* For details, go to my Web site www.linkedinworks.com/resources.htm

SendOutCards

With the economy and job markets as they are, the same way we've always been doing marketing is not enough. To be successful now, we must be creative and resourceful, and use multiple ways to market and conduct job searches. Here's how I've added something new to my marketing plan. My marketing plan now includes social networking, my e-Column, phone calls to check in and stay in touch, and sending out professional-looking cards.

Social networking with sites like LinkedIn, Facebook, Twitter and other sites gives us another opportunity to reach people who are our potential clients or who could hire us. And yet, it's still contact at a distance. The Internet has put information at our fingertips in an instant. We can find out anything we want to on the Internet 24 hours a day, 7 days a week.

What's missing is human contact and connection. That's what people are looking for now. And why they're so glad when you pick up the phone to say, "Hello". And send a greeting card on a birthday, holiday or simply to say, "I'm thinking of you."

For years I'd talk with someone or meet them, and afterwards I'd intend to send them a note saying how much I enjoyed the conversation. Yet, when it came to doing it, I never had time to go to the store to pick out a card, then to the post office to get stamps. And then mail them. So the cards didn't go out.

Now I send cards almost every day – right from my computer. Real greeting cards in an envelope with real stamps. They're *not* e-cards sent via e-mail. They're the same kind of cards that you'd buy at the store if you had time. I even sign them with my own signature. They cost less than a card that you buy at the store. I choose from thousands of cards, and find exactly the right one for the situation – birthdays, holidays, motivation and inspiration when I know someone can use a dose, congratulations on an accomplishment, and many more.

What I like best now, is that every time I go to a meeting or speak about LinkedIn, I can send a card to everyone I met. And people love the cards so much that they keep them. What does that mean for my business? Lots – people call me to tell me how much they like the card I sent, and it's up where they can see it every day. I'm on their radar screen all throughout the year.

To see how easy it is to add cards to your marketing plan, send an e-mail to me at info@linkedinworks.com and put Easy Cards in the Subject line. We'll contact you, send you a card so you can see what it's like, and then you can send out three cards to see how easy it is.

Books: These are some of my favorite books. I've read them, and go back to time and time again for more ideas. For details, and to buy these books, go to www.linkedinworks.com/resources.htm

Savvy Networking: 118 Fast & Effective Tips for Business Success – Andrea R. Nierenberg (Capital Books, Inc., 2007) Andrea Nierenberg believes that networking is about giving first. This, her third book on the subject, is a gift to all who want to turn new contacts and prospective customers into warm relationships and lifelong customers – to grow, build, and keep your business.

Networking Magic: Find the Best – from Doctors, Lawyers, and Accountants to Homes, Schools and Jobs – Rick Frishman and Jill Lublin with Mark Steisel (Adams Media, 2004). *Networking Magic* is a revolutionary concept that shows you how to find the best in all aspects of life. Whether you're looking for the most lucrative job, the highest-rated child care facility, the leading medical specialist, or virtually anything else – this is the one book that gets you on the inside track to the top experts, the highest-quality services, and the least expensive products.

The Virtual Handshake: Opening Doors and Closing Deals Online. David Teten and Scott Allen (AMACOM 2005). In *The Virtual Handshake*, David Teten and Scott Allen explain their Seven Keys to Powerful Network with clear real-life examples with you and several of your acquaintances. Review these, and think about ways you can measure and build your own network. The first five of their seven keys measure the relationship between you and your acquaintance. And two measure the size and diversity of your network.

Soft Selling in a Hard World: Plain Talk on the Art of Persuasion. Jerry Vass (Running Press 1993). *Soft Selling in a Hard World* ™ is a handbook to successful selling. Inside, you'll learn to dispel the common illusions that cost you big money, and begin to build and create your own selling moves. You'll learn specific skills to help you survive on the job, and, finally, to build your own presentation – the words, strategies, and tactics to close the sale.

Take Back your Life! Using Microsoft Office Outlook 2007 to get organized and stay organized. Sally McGhee and John Wittry (Microsoft Press 2007). Take control of the unrelenting e-mail, conflicting commitments, and endless interruptions – and take back your life! In this popular book updated for Microsoft™ Office Outlook 2007, productivity experts Sally McGhee and John Wittry show you how to reclaim what you thought you'd lost forever – your work-life balance. Now you can benefit from McGhee Productivity Solutions' highly-regarded corporate education programs, learning simple but powerful techniques for rebalancing your personal and professional commitments using Outlook 2007.

The Success Principles: How to Get from Where You Are to Where You Want to Be. Jack Canfield with Janet Switzer (A Harper Resource Book, 2005). Get ready to transform yourself for success. Jack Canfield, cocreator of the phenomenal bestselling *Chicken Soup for the Soul* ® series, turns to the principles he's studied, taught, and lived for more than 30 years in this practical and inspiring guide that will help any aspiring person get from where they are to where they want to be. The Success Principles ™ will teach you how to increase your confidence, tackle daily challenges, live with passion and purpose, and realize all your ambitions. Not merely a collection of good ideas, this book spells out the 64 timeless principles used by successful men and women throughout history.

Instant Income. Janet Switzer (McGraw-Hill 2007). Strategies That Bring in the Cash for Small Businesses, Innovative Employees, and Occasional Entrepreneurs. Instant Income is the first ever system to show you how to turn uncommon assets into income you can make and use in just hours, days or weeks – and to help you develop entirely new streams of income from unlikely sources. With Janet Switzer's proven secrets, you'll be able to discover hidden pockets of potential income – at no cost to you. Sell more to your current customers and generate new clients. Lower costs, increase prices, and maximize profits. Get others to do your marketing for you. Create your Instant Income implementation plan. Includes free online tools to build your own Instant Income® today!

Jan's LinkedIn Works! Products and Services

LinkedIn Profile Critique & Makeover – Your LinkedIn Profile is your presence on LinkedIn. You can't do anything in LinkedIn unless your Profile is up. And when someone searches and finds your Profile, they decide right then whether to connect with you, contact you, or consider you for a position or to hire you and your company. It's also your personal Web page in addition to your company site. **If people can't find you, they can't hire you.** Call me and we'll schedule your LinkedIn Profile Critique & Makeover. I give you specific steps you can do to make your LinkedIn Profile more effective so they find you. And we send you an e-mail with my recommendations and your Next Action Steps. And we can also make the revisions for you, so you don't have to.

How long have you been looking for a job? How soon do you want more clients? Every day you are looking for a job or for more clients costs you money. If your LinkedIn Profile takes only *one* day off your search, it's worth it. Call me *now* to get started. Click on the link below *now* or type it into your browser to find out more and sign up: www.linkedinworks.com/store.htm#svmo

LinkedIn Mini-Tutorial – Give me one hour and you'll be using LinkedIn to find a job of find clients … in record time. If you're conducting a job search, that's what you'll know how to do. If you want to find clients, you'll know how to do that. Simply click on the link below or type it into your browser to find out more and sign up: www.linkedinworks.com/store.htm#svmmt

LinkedIn Strategy Sessions. Consulting and Mentoring – Do you want to accomplish something in LinkedIn, and you're not quite sure how to approach it? Perhaps is conduct your job search; perhaps it's finding clients. The mechanics of LinkedIn are simple enough. You join, create your Profile, and connect with people. It's the strategies for using LinkedIn to build your business that can be challenging. **And that's exactly what I do in our Strategy Session.** I map out your best strategies for using LinkedIn.

If you want to accomplish something specific quickly, the LinkedIn Strategy Session is the perfect place to start. We'll map out Action Steps for the next 30-60 days, so you'll know exactly what to do to accomplish your goals. And we'll design your Action Steps into a time plan that fits your schedule and timeframe. The Strategy Session includes a one-hour call, a questionnaire before our call, and follow-up by e-mail. If an ongoing mentoring program makes sense to reach your goals as quickly as you want, I'll give you three options to choose from, and you choose the best way to go forward. Simply call me, click on the link below or type it into your browser to find out more www.linkedinworks.com/store.htm#svstr

Monthly LinkedIn Quick-Start Mentoring -- Quick-Start Mentoring is a monthly membership program that allows you to follow a solid, step-by-step approach to accomplishing your goals on LinkedIn. This program includes monthly coaching calls on specific topics that keep you on track for reaching your goals using LinkedIn, and field assignments to do so you make consistent progress. Monthly LinkedIn Quick-Start Mentoring is a fraction of the cost of one mentoring hour with Jan. If you want to get started with LinkedIn and really make progress, call me now. Or simply click on the link below or type it into your browser to find out more and sign up: www.linkedinworks.com/store.htm#svqs

LinkedIn Works! Teleseminars, Webinars and In-Person Seminars with your Laptop:

Find out the schedule and register now at :
- **LinkedIn for Job Searches – Find a Job in an Uncertain Job Market** - www.linkedinworks.com/store.htm#tsjob

- **LinkedIn for Entrepreneurs – Find Clients in an Uncertain Economy –** www.linkedinworks.com/store.htm#tssales

- **LinkedIn for Salespeople – Find Clients in an Uncertain Economy -** www.linkedinworks.com/store.htm#tssales

- **Your LinkedIn Profile & Mini-Tutorial --** Do people find your LinkedIn Profile? **If they don't find you, they can't hire you** or your company. You'll learn the Top 5 ways to create an effective Profile, and then you'll create or revise your own LinkedIn Profile on your laptop – www.linkedinworks.com/store.htm#tspro

For details and to register, go to www.linkedinworks.com/store.htm . Jan only does these workshops and seminars when time allows. And each one is limited to a small number of participants to be sure there's enough time for everyone.

Thank you!

Thank you for purchasing and using this book to use LinkedIn to find a job or find clients …in record time. Keep it handy so you can have a quick refresher now and again in the future when you're using LinkedIn more, and haven't used some of the features that LinkedIn offers.

When you're using LinkedIn more, and you want to make faster progress, go to www.linkedinworks.com/store.htm and sign up for your LinkedIn Mini-Tutorial, a LinkedIn Profile Critique and Makeover, a Strategy Session, or in-person seminar where you bring your laptop and learn and use LinkedIn hands-on. *Mastering LinkedIn in 7 Days or Less* is also available as an ebook, with active links. **Call me now at (877) 327-5058** to see how I can help you get the results you want. Or send an e-mail to me at: info@linkedinworks.com.

If you know people who want to find a job – or think they might be looking soon, tell them to call me right away or send an e-mail to me.

Mastering in LinkedIn in 7 Days or Less is available for purchase in quantities with special prices. They're perfect to give to:
1. Colleagues and friends who are looking for a job or think they might be looking soon, and
2. Business owners whose business has slowed down and they're looking for more clients.

For quantity purchases at special prices, contact Jan at (877) 327-5058 or by e-mail to: info@linkedinworks.com and put Quantity Books in the Subject line.

LinkedIn Works!

Make it work for you *now*

You've read and used Jan's proven strategies and tips for using LinkedIn to find a job and find clients … in record time. For more of Jan's valuable strategies, insights and easy-to-use tips, go to www.LinkedInWorks.com and sign up for **Jan's eColumn** on Social Networking for Business and LinkedIn. It's full of articles, tips, proven strategies you can do right away. .

Or call Jan at (877) 327-5058 for a 15-minute Get-Acquainted Call to see how Jan can help you do what you want to do with LinkedIn.

3070874